AF576739

This book is dedicated to the enduring spirit and lasting values of the intercollegiate game as personified by Walter Camp, the "Father of American Football."

ROSENTHAL
BROS. CO.
The
Unique

GIANT DRESS CO.
GIANT

Bank of Boston
Connecticut
has been proud to support
the efforts of the Walter Camp Football Foundation
for many years.

This year, it is a special honor
for Bank of Boston Connecticut
to mark the 100th Anniversary
of the Walter Camp All-America Football Teams
through this book.

We salute the memory of Walter Camp,
"The Father of American Football,"
and all his successors in the Foundation.

BANK OF BOSTON CONNECTICUT

A Bank of Boston Company

(Above) New Haven's Chapel Street before the Yale-Princeton game, 1904. (Page 1) Walter Camp, 1920. (Pages 2-3) Minnesota vs. Chicago. (Pages 4-5) Walter Camp (seventh from right) at the Yale coaches reunion, 1912. (Pages 6-7) Old Yale Field, 1905. (Pages 8-9) New York State Industrial Commission employees executing the Daily Dozen on the 22-story Victoria Building in New York City, 1918. (Pages 12-13) A Yale practice.

Photos on pages 14 and 28 appear courtesy of the New Haven Colony Historical Society; page 15, the Yale University Sports Information Office; and pages 110, 112-115, and 128-132, the Walter Camp Football Foundation. All remaining photos appear courtesy of the Yale University Library.

Howell Press wishes to thank Judith Ann Schiff and William R. Massa of the Yale University Library, and Debbie Sterling of the Yale University Sports Information Office, for their assistance on this project. A special thanks also goes to Carroll & Company and the Walter Camp Football Foundation. Representatives of both organizations graciously gave their time in numerous ways, but always with the goal of producing a book worthy to bear the name Walter Camp.

Designed by Carolyn Weary Brandt. Edited by Kathleen D. Valenzi. Editorial assistance provided by Cindy L. Cunningham, Ross A. Howell Jr., Jane Brown, and Christopher Daly. Text by Kathleen D. Valenzi and Michael W. Hopps.

Library of Congress Catalog Card Number 89-46285. ISBN 0-943231-21-3. Printed and bound in Japan by Dai Nippon Printing Co., Ltd. Published by Howell Press, Inc., 700 Harris Street, Suite B, Charlottesville, Virginia 22901. Telephone (804) 977-4006. First edition.

HOWELL PRESS

CHAMPION OF SPORT

The Life of Walter Camp
1859–1925

CONTENTS

An acquaintance once asked Walter Camp to name the proudest moment of his football career.

The former Yale football player—whose innovations to American college football included the scrimmage, the quarterback, the safety play, the "downs" system, team signals, and standardized scoring; who had lost only 14 games in 33 years of coaching Yale football—gave the question some thought.

His happiest moment, he recalled, took place during his captaincy of the Yale football team. A player kept breaking training rules, and after a time, Camp felt compelled to drop him from the team. The other players objected. After a heated argument, Camp resigned. The next day, a humble team returned, agreed that his decision should be upheld, and invited Camp to resume as their captain.

It was a simple matter of integrity and team support, but it meant more to the father of American football than anything else.

Hopkins Grammar School. Walter Camp graduated from this New Haven, Connecticut, preparatory school in 1876.

A MAN FOR ALL SEASONS

On April 7, 1859, a seemingly insignificant event occurred in the small Connecticut town of New Britain. There, Ellen Cornwall Camp gave birth to a son. She and her husband, Leverett Lee Camp, named him Walter Chauncey. While his birth occasioned little fuss outside of the New Britain community, Walter Chauncey Camp was destined to become one of America's favorite sons.

Following the death of Walter's maternal grandfather in New Britain in 1863, the Camps moved to New Haven. A picturesque town noted for its broad elm-tree-lined streets, New Haven is located approximately 40 miles south of New Britain on the Connecticut coast.

An educator, Leverett Camp became the principal of New Haven's Washington School and, later, the Dwight School. While the senior Camp never drew a large salary, he owned several pieces of property in New Britain and Meriden, Connecticut, as well as a summer home on Martha's Vineyard in Massachusetts, so the Camps had a comfortable lifestyle. Walter's mother, Ellen, became a favorite among her son's friends for the chocolate cakes that she served when they visited. She loved poetry and passed that passion on to her son, who also acquired her high ideals of morality, honesty, and integrity.

When Walter reached school age, his parents enrolled him in Hopkins Grammar School, a preparatory school of national repute. Hopkins dates back to 1657, when Edward Hopkins, the second governor of the Connecticut Colony, died and bequeathed money for a school "for the breeding up of hopefull youths." In June 1660 Hopkins opened for its first academic session in

Walter Camp in his preparatory school uniform.

a building at the corner of High and Wall Streets (the location of the present Yale Law School). Originally intended to prepare young boys for entrance to Harvard in Massachusetts, in 1701 Hopkins became allied with New Haven's new Collegiate School, the forerunner of Yale College. In fact, Elihu Yale, the college's first private benefactor for whom the Collegiate School was renamed in 1718, was the nephew of Anne Yale Hopkins, wife of the governor.

From the start, Walter excelled academically, earning high marks in Latin, Greek, and mathematics. During his enrollment, William L. Cushing, a former star rower for Yale, served as rector. Cushing's administration was marked by one of the highest attendance rates in the history of the school. As Hopkins possessed no dormitories, all of the 220 boys either lived at home, as did Walter, or roomed out at the houses of various New Haven residents.

Over the years, Walter grew into a tall, lean youth. He loved to compete, particularly in sports, but his slender physique put him at a disadvantage. Possessing strong will power and perseverance, Walter began building himself up through daily exercise in order to gain speed, agility, and endurance. In the evenings New Haven residents would see him jogging along their streets.

Baseball originally dominated fall sports at Hopkins. In 1875 the Hopkins baseball team challenged the local New Haven high school team to a game. By the end of the eighth inning, the high school team led the game, 10 to 9, but Walter's curve ball proved too much for the opposition. Hopkins left the field victorious.

Cold weather and a dearth of rival teams soon ended the fall baseball season at Hopkins. Football replaced it, and Walter couldn't have been happier. To young Camp, football was the supreme sport, and no doubt the round, black rubber ball that he played with at Hopkins whenever an opportunity presented itself was among his most prized possessions. Because of the close alliance between the preparatory school and Yale, the boys at Hopkins avidly followed Yale athletics. Walter's favorite, of course, was Yale football.

As an adult, Camp would recall a game played in 1873 between the Yale Bulldogs and the "Eton eleven," a team captained by an Eton man and comprising Englishmen from New York City.

> "The score card impressed us greatly," he wrote in *American Football*, "for there was a marquis on the team; there was also on the English team one of the tallest men we had ever seen on the football field. His height was given me after the game as six feet, seven inches, and he certainly looked all of this. When he punted the ball with that long leg of his, it seemed as though it would never stop going."

Watching such fine playing, Walter yearned for the opportunity to one day don the blue and join the ranks of his college football heroes.

But in order for that dream to become reality, first Walter needed to pass the rigid entrance examinations required for admission to Yale. Together with his peers from Hopkins, Walter sat for exams a few days before his

1876 commencement. To the anxious boys, the straight-backed chairs and formidable examination room at Yale College were imposing, but no more so than the Yale professors and tutors who individually questioned each young candidate. Walter needed to prove his knowledge of Greek and Latin, both reading and grammar, as well as arithmetic, English grammar, and geography in order to be accepted at the college.

Much to his delight, Camp learned that he had passed. After a summer of high expectation, he joined the ranks of the 1876 Yale freshman class.

Compared to the strict discipline of Hopkins, Yale must have seemed invigorating to Camp, even liberating. Student enrollment at Yale College numbered well above 750 students, and many were eager to introduce the new freshman to the customs of the college.

If Camp's first night was like that of Yale freshmen before him, his initiation into Yale traditions began immediately. That evening junior classmen marched beneath freshman dormitory windows shouting the Yale cheer and inviting the newcomers to a rush at Hopkins Grammar School. Few freshmen resisted the call, and Camp undoubtedly found himself on the playing field of his old alma mater awaiting the contest. There, the freshmen came face to face with sophomores, who, with arms encircling one another's waists, began pushing the freshmen backwards. Once the freshmen understood what was going on, they clustered likewise, and the two classes proceeded to jostle each other back and forth. Only the bravest freshmen voluntarily took a place in the front lines of the "push rush." Those who did

(Above) *An examination room in Yale's Alumni Hall, 1879. Entrance exams to Yale College were administered in rooms like this one.* **(Overleaf, pages 18-19)** *Old South College and the Yale fence, 1874. A part of "Brick Row," the original Yale College, South College was one of several buildings torn down in the late 1800s to make room for more modern structures. The fence, also uprooted, received a new home within the campus quadrangle.*

A typical student's room, South College. Yale's old residence colleges contained 32 chambers, each featuring a main sitting room, washroom, two bedrooms, a clothes press, and a coal closet.

The old pump, 1870. Like the Yale fence, the pump served as a gathering place for games, songs, and pranks. These locations, as much as structured study halls, taught students the value of strength, wit, opinion, loyalty, camaraderie, and sport.

Walter Camp playing golf. Although football was his first love, Camp excelled in many sports. An avid golfer, he co-authored a book on the subject, Drives and Putts, *with Lilian Brooks.*

often went on to earn honors on the Yale football team. Walter Camp no doubt joined his more stalwart classmates front and center.

During his first year at Yale, Camp joined Delta Kappa, an academic society for freshmen. Otherwise, Camp and his first-year classmates faced many restrictions imposed by tradition. Even if he had wanted to in his freshman year, Camp could not smoke a pipe on the street or on campus, carry a cane before Washington's Birthday, dance at the Junior Class Promenade, or sit on the famous Yale fence.

With so many social restrictions, no wonder Camp immersed himself in sports. At Yale, he became a champion swimmer at both long and short distances. He played tennis, wrestled, and rowed with the crew team. He ran track and invented the running hurdle-step, a method of clearing a hurdle without having first to halt one's forward movement. He captained and pitched for the baseball team and was one of the first to throw an effective curveball. He also played shortstop and had seasons leading his league in both fielding percentage and batting average. His talents on the baseball diamond would lead in 1884 to an invitation from the National League of Baseball Clubs to join their staff of league umpires. It was an honor that he would decline, for his first love was and always would be football.

The 1876 Yale baseball team. One of only eight men in college baseball at the time to pitch a one-hitter, Walter Camp (back row, second from left) led the league in batting averages and was captain of the freshman team. He later received an offer to pitch for the New York Giants, which he turned down.

During his sophomore year, Camp joined the He Boule' academic society and, a year later, the Delta Kappa Epsilon fraternity.

Junior year witnessed the arrival of the Promenade, a formal dance that had evolved out of Yale College's old

(Above) *During Walter Camp's senior year at Yale, light-hearted tunes like "Cradle's Empty and the Baby's Gone," "Five-Cent Shave," and "Never Take the Horseshoe From the Door" were popular.* **(Facing)** *Thanksgiving Jubilee, 1876. Sponsored by the freshman class, the jubilee took the form of burlesque entertainment. The faculty of Yale College eventually abolished the annual event due to its somewhat immoral nature.*

Wooden Spoon celebration, and Tap Day, when the highly selective senior societies—Skull and Bones and Scroll and Key—announced which members of the junior class would be invited to join their ranks.

When Tap Day arrived late in May of his junior year in 1879, Camp and his classmates gathered near the Yale fence. Meanwhile, individual members of the respective societies departed their halls at intervals of two to four minutes and, with due pomp and ceremony, crossed the campus to the waiting assembly.

To Camp's delight, a Skull and Bones member pushed through the gathering, slapped him on the back, and said aloud, "Go to your room." With all eyes on him, Camp led the society man to his dormitory, where in formal language, the senior announced Camp's election to the prestigious 15-member society.

To his credit, given the extent of his social and athletic activities, Walter never forgot the primary purpose of his enrollment at Yale—to receive an education. He was an excellent student who met head on the challenges of Cicero, Tacitus, Plato, and Thucydides, as well as studies on astronomy and natural philosophy.

During his senior year, Camp won both the Ivy Ode and Class Poem competitions. But those honors must have paled when compared to the privilege of being able to sit on the section of the Yale fence that faced Chapel Street, the exclusive domain of senior classmen.

Along Yale's legendary fence scholars and athletes mingled, learned to respect the others' strengths and weaknesses. From issues of politics to affairs of the heart, the conversations inspired by the fence lingered in the

memories of the school's alumni long after the fence was torn down in 1888 to make way for a building.

From such an esteemed vantage point Camp viewed the busy New Haven community, while behind him stretched Yale's beautiful Green, the brick buildings of old college row, and a grove of stately elms. For seniors, the fence marked the boundary between the familiar world of academics and the new, challenging world of business. It seemed a fitting place for the thoughtful Camp, whose undergraduate days were nearing an end.

Yale Medical School laboratory. After studying anatomy, surgery, and treatment of disease for two years at Yale, Walter Camp abandoned his medical pursuits. He had discovered that he could not bear the sight of blood.

In 1881 Camp entered Yale Medical School. The previous year, the medical college had changed the length of its program from two years to three. Academic years stretched from six months to nine, and exams became mandatory for graduation. The change, later adopted by other colleges, proved so taxing for the students that more than 60 percent of those enrolled that year left the program. The mass exodus from Yale Medical School didn't intimidate Camp.

Chartered in 1810, making it the fifth oldest medical school in America, as well as Yale's oldest professional school, Yale Medical School seemed a natural choice to an athlete with a life-long interest in the body and its development. Over the next two years, Camp immersed himself in his studies and passed all but two subjects that he needed in order to receive his degree. Then, to the surprise of his family, friends, and professors, he withdrew from the program. In later years, when asked why he had left Yale Medical School, Camp gave two different reasons: to most people he said that the death of a surgeon with whom he'd intended

Ambulance at Yale College.

to practice resulted in his decision; to a close friend, he confided that he disliked the sight of blood, an ironic statement for one who loved the nineteenth-century game of football.

After leaving school in 1882, Camp joined the sales staff of the New York City branch of the Manhattan Watch Company. A year later, he took a similar job with the New York office of The New Haven Clock Company, one of the largest manufacturers in Connecticut at that time. Eventually the company promoted him through the ranks to assistant treasurer and transferred him to the main office in New Haven. His rise within the company continued as Camp progressed from treasurer to general manager in 1902, president in 1903, and several years later, chairman of the board. In the meantime, the young clock company executive had made the acquaintance of Alice Graham Sumner, the principal of the Welch School, a New Haven teacher's college, and sister of one of Yale's most distinguished professors, sociologist William Graham Sumner. In a touching letter to the professor dated August 30, 1886, Camp asked for Alice's hand in marriage. William Sumner gave his blessings, and the couple wed on June 30, 1888.

Alice Camp proved an exceptional partner to the man who now served as Yale's unpaid football coach, but whose business commitments prevented him from watching the team's daily practices. A fan of the sport herself, "Allie" walked the sidelines of the football field during practices and took copious notes of the day's activities. These she shared with her husband, who reviewed them each evening.

(Above) *Walter Camp's residence, 1888 to 1905. This Gill Street cottage became a haven for undergraduate officials and athletes who sought Camp's advice on strategies for upcoming games. Frequently, furniture was moved aside so Camp could demonstrate new plays.* **(Facing)** *The New Haven Clock Company, World War I.*

Alice Graham Sumner Camp with her mother. When Camp married Alice Sumner in 1888, he acquired an invaluable asset. She spent more time taking notes on the sidelines at football practices than her husband, the team's unofficial coach, whose work that year prevented him from monitoring the Bulldogs's daily progress.

Their Gill Street home became a haven for Yale football players and undergraduate officials, who frequently sought out Camp's advice on techniques and strategies for upcoming games. On the days that Yale played against Harvard or Princeton in New Haven, it was not uncommon to find as many as 250 to 300 guests gathering at their house for a pre-game lunch. "Mrs. Walter," as Alice Camp was frequently called, earned the respect and affection of all who met her.

Walter and Alice Camp first became parents in 1891, when their son, Walter Camp Jr., was born. During his lifetime, the junior Camp would distinguish himself on the football field, as well as the deadly battlegrounds of the first world war, and later settle into the life of a successful film executive in California. In 1917 he and his first wife, the former Frances English, produced the Camp's only grandchild, also a son, named Walter Camp III.

Janet Camp, the second and last child born to Walter and Alice, arrived in 1897. As an adult, Janet would one day amass nearly 3,300 documents pertaining to the art and literature of the pre-Raphaelites, such as Dante Gabriel Rossetti, Christina Rossetti, and W. Holman Hunt. The collection, considered the finest in the country, was acquired by Princeton in 1971.

The Camps were a popular couple and had many friends. Ironically, one of Walter's best friends was Lorin F. Deland, head coach at Harvard who developed the football play known as the "Flying Wedge" that astonished the Yale team when it was first used against them in 1892. The rival coaches got along so well that in 1896,

(Above) *Walter Camp with his daughter Janet, 1913.* **(Overleaf, pages 32-33)** *Walter Camp Jr. running for a touchdown, 1910. The junior Walter, like his father, played halfback for Yale College.*

Walter Camp III. The Camps's only grandchild, Walter III was born in 1917 to Walter Jr. and his first wife, the former Frances English.

they collaborated on a book, *Football,* published by Houghton, Mifflin & Company.

As was the case with Deland, many of Walter's friends were involved in athletics of one form or another. Other friendships grew out of the many business and civic activities in which he participated. Besides overseeing Yale athletics and the daily operation of The New Haven Clock Company, Camp also served at various times as president of the New Haven Civic Federation, board member of the Serbian Relief Fund, and chairman of the Chamber of Commerce's Recreation Committee and Welfare Committee.

Not surprisingly, when the alma mater of his youth, Hopkins Grammar School, found itself in dire financial straits, Camp offered to lend a hand. Since his days there, the school had experienced a steady decline in enrollment, owing in part to an old-fashioned curriculum. Finances became strained to the point that teachers often went unpaid for long periods of time. The preparatory school could no longer count on its reputation to ensure a minimum number of students.

In 1900 Hopkins' trustees elected Walter Camp and another alumnus, Henry W. Farnam, to replace two men who had recently resigned. Both men were astonished to find out how desperate the situation had become and began to look for ways to put the school in the black.

Three years later, Camp was elected as Hopkins' secretary treasurer. Immediately, he instituted a policy whereby detailed reports of the financial status of the school were sent to the trustees before each board meeting so that informed decisions could be made

Walter Camp with his son, 1918. Both Camps honorably served their country during World War I. The senior became athletic director of U.S. Navy and U.S. Army Air Service training camps. Walter Jr. entered the war as an infantryman, rose to the rank of captain, received five citations for conspicuous military service, and was gassed in three major battles: Belleau Wood, Château-Thierry, and the Argonne.

promptly. He personally oversaw expenditures, which resulted in even more detailed reports. After a thorough analysis of the school's finances, which revealed a $773.13 deficit for 1903, Camp put into action a financial program that called for the immediate collection of small donations to meet the school's debts, followed by a fund-raising campaign aimed at wealthy alumni, who were encouraged to contribute generous endowments. Facing the board with his plan, an empassioned Camp said:

> I dislike extremely to have such an unpleasant story to tell, but it seems to me it is best for us to face it at once and to take counsel as to what our course of action should be as trustees. I do not think I go too far in saying that the school ought not to run as it has been; that is, on such a close margin that the teachers' salaries have been behind; that it is so difficult to make both ends meet that the Treasurer is obliged from time to time to advance small sums, and that everything like provision for the future in the way of keeping the plant up to its highest state of efficiency, is certainly impossible.

Inspired by Camp's efforts, the trustees enacted further changes at Hopkins, including revising the school's calendar to correspond with Yale's and revising the curriculum to accommodate new college entrance requirements.

Even so, the fate of Hopkins hung in the balance for many years, as contributors were slow to sign on. The situation became critical enough that the trustees seriously contemplated merging Hopkins with the New Haven high school. In fact Camp himself signed a draft for such a merger with Connecticut's Governor Simeon E. Baldwin. After considerable debate, the proposed merger was abandoned in April 1912, and Hopkins sold its property and moved to a temporary location on Chapel Street. Luckily, the tide began to turn, and in the years that followed, alumni stepped forward to provide the school's desperately needed funding.

Camp was no stranger to institutional finances. As treasurer of the Yale Financial Union, he developed a system where one athletic treasury funded all Yale sports. Over a ten-year period, the fund accumulated a surplus of more than $100,000. Proceeds collected from ticket sales to football games attributed to the health of the fund and were used to support the college's less popular sports.

For 15 years Camp also served as the treasurer of Yale Field. He became chairman of the college's athletic committee and a graduate advisor in athletics. In all, his involvement with Yale sports spanned 25 years. Recognizing his long-term advisory role, in 1908 Yale College administrators awarded Camp an honorary Master of Arts degree.

Had Camp never done another thing, he would still have accomplished more than most people aspire to. But despite his successes as a student, businessman, husband, parent, civil servant, athletic advisor, and trustee, Camp would be remembered best for singlehandedly revolutionizing the game of college football.

Walter Camp wore many hats. Besides coaching the Bulldogs and directing Yale athletics for years, he became a well-known sports columnist and author, served as trustee and treasurer of Hopkins Grammar School, and chaired the recreation and welfare committees of the New Haven Chamber of Commerce.

WALTER CAMP.

In baseball, football, and every game,
  Your name is known to all.
Athletic adviser of all Yale sports,
  You answer to the call.
As business man you too excel;
  You're a winner in each line.
There's a friendly thought for you each hour,
  As your clocks point out the time.

Manhattan Field, December 7, 1893. Princeton is about to attack the Yale defensive line with a wedge play before a crowd of 50,000.

FATHER OF AMERICAN FOOTBALL

The year Walter Camp was born, Charles Darwin published his *Origin of Species*. The coincidence is fitting, because in the long history of sport, Camp, more than any other man, put the theory of evolution into practice.

Before he had turned voting age, Camp had conceived many of the rules changes that transfigured the game of rugby and laid the foundation for modern American football. Throughout his life, he would cultivate football and welcome intelligent changes that were the brainchildren of others. He accepted minimal credit for his ideas. The father of American football knew the game was bigger than he was.

Camp had developed a reputation for fairness and good sportsmanship. He valued honor above all else, especially on the playing field. To Camp, self-control and the ability to accept defeat graciously were as important to athletes as physical build. The fictional Frank Merriwell, hero of numerous sports stories and the ideal of sportsmanship, is said to have been modeled on Camp. His reputation for fairness might best have been expressed when Princeton selected Camp to referee its 1885 contest against his alma mater, Yale.

In the nineteenth century, football was considered an outlaw game. Thanks largely to Camp's innovations, the sport achieved a popularity that has never stopped expanding. Football was a common spectacle on nearly every college campus in the 1840s and '50s. Unorganized matches of the game Americans call soccer materialized spontaneously. But the enthusiasm generated often turned to violence. Wrote a pair of

Walter Camp (back row, fourth from left) and the 1876 Yale Varsity Football Team. The first Yale team to play "American" football, the 1876 eleven held their games at New Haven's Hamilton Park and the cricket grounds in Hoboken, New Jersey. Yale was the victor in each of the year's three contests, defeating Harvard 1-0, Princeton 2-0, and Columbia 2-0.

Yale underclassmen in the early 1850s:

> There were yellings and shoutings and
> wiping of noses,
> Where the hue of the lily has changed to
> the rose's,
> There were tearing of shirts, and ripping
> of stitches,
> and breaches of peaces, and pieces
> of britches.

Many schools decided to prohibit their students from engaging in this deleterious diversion. Yale banned campus games in 1859, as did Harvard the next year. Neither lifted its ban until 1871.

The first intercollegiate American football game featured Princeton and Rutgers and took place in New Brunswick, New Jersey, on Saturday, November 6, 1869. Camp was ten years old. About 100 spectators watched the men take the field. The red stocking-caps some of the Rutgers players wore were the only semblance of a uniform for either team. Slowing for a moment on his way past, an elderly bicyclist bellowed, "You men will come to no decent Christian end."

Part rugby and part soccer, played with a spherical ball, the game allowed 25 players to a side. The two captains, who would act as the game's goalkeepers, agreed at the outset to keep violence to a minimum. The game would last until one side scored six goals. Players were permitted to use their hands but not to pick up the ball and run with it.

A coin toss gave Princeton the ball and Rutgers the wind. Rutgers scored the first goal and ultimately prevailed, six goals to four. The next week they met again, and Princeton won the rematch. It wasn't until 1874, however, when Montreal's McGill University sent a team to Massachusetts to play Harvard, that an intercollegiate match occurred that most historians agree was football—with the earmarks of the game we know today. The 1869 game was more like soccer; the McGill-Harvard meeting, more akin to rugby and a closer ally to modern football. It ended in a scoreless tie.

Harvard had to schedule games with the Canadian university because it couldn't find an American school willing to play its brand of ball. Princeton, Yale, Rutgers, and others preferred the soccer-style game. But in 1875 the Crimson persuaded Yale to engage them in rugby football. Some Princeton players sat in attendance and liked what they saw.

The nation's centennial saw the formation of the Intercollegiate Football Association (IFA). Harvard, Yale, and Princeton became charter members, and The Big Three agreed to play the rugby-style game. The association's other significant decision was to change the shape of the ball, from round to oblong.

When Camp entered Yale in the fall of 1876, football was being played on a spacious field 140 yards long by 70 yards wide. Players wore no pads and only knitted caps for headgear. The game was divided into two 45-minute halves. There were no time-outs for huddles. Players ran until they dropped or were too badly injured to continue. Fist fights were commonplace. Activities such as jumping on a prostrate opponent went unsupervised. The number of players to a side had been

"Out of the Game" from Harper's Weekly. *With the growing popularity and use of mass-formation plays from 1888 to 1896, football injuries and fatalities reached alarming numbers.*

reduced to 15, but there were no substitutions. After "minor" injuries, players remained on the field. If an injured player left, his mates played shorthanded.

An outstanding multi-sport athlete, Camp had natural ability but never took it for granted. It was through rigorous exercises that he built himself up to a football player's weight.

Camp put his talents on display immediately his freshman year at Yale, earning a starting position at halfback. But his talents weren't restricted to running. He punted, drop-kicked, and place-kicked. In the 1876 Thanksgiving Day game against Princeton, he threw the first forward pass on record. It was controversial, but it went for a touchdown. At the time, Camp was seventeen years old.

Walter Camp at the Yale fence, 1880. Having a picture taken alone in uniform at the Yale fence was the sole privilege of team captains, such as Camp, who led the Bulldogs through three seasons.

As a Yale sophomore, Camp attended the IFA's 1877 rules convention. For the most part, he kept quiet and observed.

His powers of observation and extraordinary memory (from adolescence on, he could recite dozens of poems in full) made him a natural strategist. Before his junior year, Camp's teammates elected him captain. They would elect him captain each successive year of his college career, though one season he would step aside so his friend Franklin Eaton could assume the role.

Camp attended the 1878 rules convention, held at the Massasoit House in Springfield, Massachusetts. Believing the number of players on a team made for a shoving match, he suggested it be reduced to 11. The association voted the notion down.

Camp was resolute. At the following year's con-

Walter Camp (front row, second from right) and the 1881 Yale Varsity Football Team. While Harvard outscored Yale in 1881, a strange rule awarded victory to the Bulldogs for scoring four fewer safeties. Yale finished the season with a 5-1-0 record.

Missouri vs. Nebraska. Eastern dominance in football diminished in the early 1900s with the advent of the forward pass. While midwestern coaches developed a variety of winning passing plays, the Ivy Leagues persistently stuck to the running game.

vention, he repeated the suggestion. Along with it, he proposed the safety as a scoring play. To this time, a team could retreat with the ball behind its goal line with impunity. Camp argued that the defensive team should be awarded points for compelling the offensive team back that far. Neither suggestion was accepted.

It may have been during these three conventions that Camp developed his technique of argument. His method was to allow other delegates to talk first, let them all debate to the point of exhaustion, until someone inevitably wondered why Camp hadn't offered an opinion. At that point he would speak his mind.

The 1880 convention took place on October 12, again in Springfield. Camp had by now gained considerable respect among his fellow conventioneers for his eloquent speech and gallant manner—not to mention his achievements on the field. For the third time he proffered that the number of players be reduced from 15 to 11, and this time his peers agreed. For the second time, he suggested the safety as a scoring play. The delegates agreed. Also on that day he proposed the most dramatic and important rules change in football history. He introduced the football scrimmage, in opposition to the rugby scrum.

In the scrum no team had continuous possession of the ball. It was set on the field, and both teams fought for it, as in a hockey face-off. Players clustered around the ball, locked arms, kicked at it, and attempted to drive it free from the flock of bodies. Occasionally, a man would trap the ball between his heels, jump in the air, and try to hurl it away from the others. Often several minutes passed before the ball rolled to the open field.

Camp saw this as a disorderly way to play a game, feeling it relied on chance. It made football difficult for spectators to follow, and he felt certain that the sport could never achieve popularity unless it offered a different method of beginning play.

The scrimmage formation would give one team undisputed possession of the ball. The team controlling the football at the play's end brought it back into play when the game resumed. "The man who first receives the ball from the snap-back," clarified Camp, "shall be called the quarterback, and shall not rush forward under penalty of foul." This would allow a team to develop and implement a plan of attack, whereas the scrum's randomness left little opportunity for strategy.

The other convention delegates saw his point. All wanted their outlaw game's reputation to change. They admitted the innovation would render the sport far more accessible for the common fan.

This time they didn't wait another year to reconsider Camp's idea. Despite a good deal of preliminary argument, they voted the idea through unanimously.

Modern football begins with the invention of the scrimmage. There have been countless rules changes since then. The size of the field has been reduced to 100 yards by 53⅓ yards. The goal posts have moved. The number of points awarded for various achievements, the fouls, and accompanying penalties have changed. Any of these could change again. But the scrimmage clearly distinguishes American football from its rugby and soccer ancestry. Every other rule is a technicality.

(Above) *Fans en route to the Yale-Princeton Thanksgiving Day game in New York City, 1893.* **(Overleaf, pages 46-47)** *The "Minnesota Shift," Minnesota vs. Nebraska. Devised by Minnesota coach Harry Williams, a former pupil of Walter Camp, the "shift" proved so devastating to defenses that, once again, cries to abolish mass plays were heard across the country.*

Football's earliest fans. With millionaires, politicians, writers, and socialites withstanding the cold to watch the annual contest, the Thanksgiving Day game became a major social event that few missed.

Yale athletic chairman Walter Camp (left) with Mike Murphy, the University of Pennsylvania's athletic trainer and the preeminent track coach of his time.

Of course, the scrimmage created a new set of problems. If a team had undisputed control of the ball, it lost possession only if it fumbled or chose to kick. Camp assumed that a team unable to advance the ball would do the sportsmanlike thing and punt.

The sportsman Camp didn't fully grasp the dimensions of competitive fire. When the new season began in 1880, a team could hold the ball an entire half, and then the opponent, after accepting the second-half kickoff, could hold it for the rest of the game. Fourth down (a term not yet invented) meant nothing at all, because it was followed by fifth down, and sixth, then fifteenth and thirtieth.

In fact, in the Thanksgiving Day Princeton-Yale game that year, Princeton held the ball the entire first half. There was only one kick. It occurred in the second half and was made by Walter Camp.

A knee injury ended Camp's playing days in 1881. He became Yale's advisory coach, was in fact the first to use a clipboard. He was not technically a coach, however, since in those days a team's only engineer was its captain. When captains made notes for their successors, strategy sifted through the generations.

In 1882 Camp introduced the concept of downs and yards to be gained. A down was a play from scrimmage, ending either when a player had run out of bounds or had been tackled. The team had three downs to advance the ball five yards or yield possession to the opponent. However, if it were to lose ten yards in its three downs, it also kept the ball, since such an event was attributed to fine defensive effort. If the defense continued to push

Yale's Ted Coy kicking a field goal, 1910. The kicking game played a major role in the strategy of early college football. Running plays were difficult and tedious, making the field goal the more popular means of scoring.

the offensive team backward toward the latter's own goal, Camp didn't deem it adverse to the defensive 11 to remain without the ball. The IFA instituted the idea. To facilitate tracking the yardage, Camp suggested white lines be drawn across the width of the field at five-yard intervals. Thus the "gridiron" was born.

Camp also saw the necessity of signals, so the offensive 11 could act in tandem while masking their intentions from the defensive team. The quarterback would shout an entire sentence to his teammates, and his omission of a word or a few words indicated specific individual assignments regarding the play his team was about to run. This led to play-calling in the huddle and, much later, to the system of number-calling the John Elways and Randall Cunninghams of today use at the scrimmage line.

In the early 1880s some schools used rugby's scoring system, while others made up new sets of scoring rules before each game. Most of the western schools counted touchdowns six points. Some of the eastern schools awarded them only one. Several schools gave touchdowns and field goals the same value, perhaps four points or five, while many scored them differently. At the Ivy League schools, a field goal was worth more than a touchdown. Clearly, the scoring system needed to be standardized.

When discerning the proper value of each method of scoring, Camp first tried to look to posterity. He guessed the future of the game would lie in running the ball rather than kicking it. He decided a touchdown would be about twice as hard to score as a field goal, and that the former should be worth six points to the latter's three. However, he thought intercollegiate football wasn't ready for such an extreme change. Time would reveal the perfect system.

For now, standardization was the important thing, and Camp obtained enactment for the following scoring system in 1883: five points for a field goal, two for a touchdown, four for a successful conversion on the kick after the touchdown, and one point for a safety.

After Camp's four years of undergraduate school, he proceeded directly to Yale Medical School, where he excelled. Following his second year at the medical school, he confided to his friend Walter Jennings that he was going to quit his studies. He had decided to pursue a business career.

Jennings was thunderstruck. He knew quite well Camp's record in medical school and how close Camp was, at that very moment, to becoming a doctor. "You can't mean," he said to Camp, "to throw it up after all your study."

Camp allowed that he meant precisely that. Jennings demanded an explanation.

"The fact is that I can't bear the sight of blood."

No sideline onlooker could listen to the grunts emerging from the throats of men crashing at full running speed into others, watch the constant injuries that inevitably occur in each game, and deny that football is brutal. In Camp's time it was more brutal, even bloodier than today. But the hemophobe Camp, a man with an abundance of interests, didn't refute allegations that this one bizarre interest of his was uncivilized.

As college football's popularity increased, so did the number of odes written in its honor:

"The Gridiron Mother"
A health to the Gridiron, bless her!
She's a mother that's making men;
She turns out none that are weaklings,
She trains them as she can.
And her lads they grow up sturdy,
Their jaws they are undershot,
And when she gets them ready
They're a rugged fighting lot.

They never whine or whimper;
You may beat them till they blink,
But their grip you can't pry open,
When once their teeth they sink.
So here's to the Gridiron Mother,
And her "downs" and "yards of ten;"
For her lads are worth the raising,
This mother that's making men!

(Overleaf, pages 54-55) *Michigan vs. Pennsylvania.*

Swarthmore vs. Brown. In American football's infancy, field goals earned more points than touchdowns.

"The average American has a strain in his blood coming down to him through rugged ancestors that gives him that unquenchable lust for uncivilized places," Camp once stated, concluding his remarks by relating part of a street-corner conversation he had with his friend Frederic Remington, the great western painter and a former Yale player.

"Camp," the artist asked him, "you're not going to civilize the only real thing we have left, are you?"

Princeton's 11 first developed a play, later perfected by Harvard, called the "V-trick," or "Flying Wedge." At kickoff, the kicking team lined up in a V-formation, with everyone but the kicker standing several yards behind the scrimmage line. Right before he kicked the ball, the kicker's teammates got a running start toward the line. The kicker nudged the ball forward and play began—with all the offense in forward motion and the defense awaiting them ten yards away. The kicker picked up the ball, and his teammates scrambled to get in front of him. The ball carrier now within the crick of a V-formation, his team proceeded down the field. In a pyramid effect, the defensive team had to beat one man, then two, and the two coming after that felt like four.

In a variant form of the flying wedge, players sewed suitcase handles onto their pant legs. One man grabbed the handles on the player in front of him, who in turn locked his hands onto a teammate before him, and a chain of blockers steamrolled down the field with the ball carrier behind them, flattening defenders.

Soon every team made use of the flying wedge. Injuries mounted exponentially. Camp, no prude when

(Above and overleaf, pages 58-59) *The "Flying Wedge." Lorin F. Deland, a military scholar and Harvard's coach, applied Napoleon's principle on the concentration of military force to the basic wedge play and created the "Flying Wedge."* **(Overleaf, pages 60-61)** *Princeton breaks through the Yale line with the "Revolving Tandem," 1897. In tandem plays one player, usually a back, precedes the ball carrier and bulldozes a path through the defensive line. This may have been a precursor to the modern blocking back.*

BUY A SCORE CARD
WATCH BOARD
10
8 NORTH STAND

Yale vs. Carlisle at the New York City Polo Grounds. The Carlisle Indians under Coach "Pop" Warner were known for their trickery. In 1903 Carlisle ends appliquéd padded footballs to their jerseys in order to fool opponents as to who had the ball.

it came to violence, abhorred this proliferation of brutality. Even more, he vehemently objected to the callous disregard such antics made of the notion of honor and fair play on the gridiron. In 1885 he suggested the game's first penalty, and it passed. The penalty was for offsides—crossing the scrimmage line before the snap from center. Players and officials ignored the rule.

A rule Camp suggested allowing tackling below the waist, to as low as the knees, met with success. It meant to favor the defense and, combined with the new rule prohibiting linemen from blocking with extended arms, it spawned the close-order formation. Linemen closed ranks, and the T-formation was born.

Camp became Yale's first field coach in 1888, the year before he selected his first All-America Team. Despite the long hours he now worked at The New Haven Clock Company, Camp continued to coach Yale through 1892. But he had help.

> "In 1888, Yale actually had *two* coaches," Yale guard William "Pudge" Heffelfinger told sportswriter Jack McCallum, "Camp and his earnest bride, Allie.... They were newlyweds and Walter was sales manager in the New York office of the New Haven Clock Company. His superiors wouldn't let him attend our afternoon practices, so he sent his wife to stand in for him. I can still see her pacing up and down the sideline, taking notes of our scrimmages. Walter kept in touch with our progress by reading her notebook. Then, several nights a week, some of us on the team

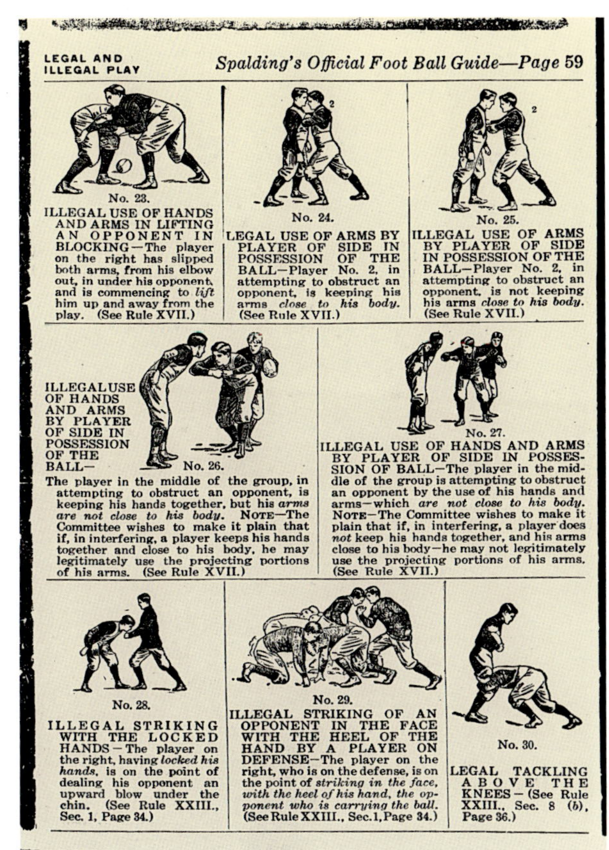

LEGAL AND ILLEGAL PLAY

Spalding's Official Foot Ball Guide—Page 59

No. 23.

ILLEGAL USE OF HANDS AND ARMS IN LIFTING AN OPPONENT IN BLOCKING—The player on the right has slipped both arms, from his elbow out, in under his opponent, and is commencing to *lift* him up and away from the play. (See Rule XVII.)

No. 24.

LEGAL USE OF ARMS BY PLAYER OF SIDE IN POSSESSION OF THE BALL—Player No. 2, in attempting to obstruct an opponent, is keeping his arms *close to his body.* (See Rule XVII.)

No. 25.

ILLEGAL USE OF ARMS BY PLAYER OF SIDE IN POSSESSION OF THE BALL—Player No. 2, in attempting to obstruct an opponent, is not keeping his arms *close to his body.* (See Rule XVII.)

No. 26.

ILLEGAL USE OF HANDS AND ARMS BY PLAYER OF SIDE IN POSSESSION OF THE BALL—The player in the middle of the group, in attempting to obstruct an opponent, is keeping his hands together, but his *arms are not close to his body.* NOTE—The Committee wishes to make it plain that if, in interfering, a player keeps his hands together and close to his body, he may legitimately use the projecting portions of his arms. (See Rule XVII.)

No. 27.

ILLEGAL USE OF HANDS AND ARMS BY PLAYER OF SIDE IN POSSESSION OF BALL—The player in the middle of the group is attempting to obstruct an opponent by the use of his hands and arms—which *are not close to his body.* NOTE—The Committee wishes to make it plain that if, in interfering, a player does *not* keep his hands together, and his arms close to his body—he may not legitimately use the projecting portions of his arms. (See Rule XVII.)

No. 28.

ILLEGAL STRIKING WITH THE LOCKED HANDS—The player on the right, having *locked his hands*, is on the point of dealing his opponent an upward blow under the chin. (See Rule XXIII., Sec. 1, Page 34.)

No. 29.

ILLEGAL STRIKING OF AN OPPONENT IN THE FACE WITH THE HEEL OF THE HAND BY A PLAYER ON DEFENSE—The player on the right, who is on the defense, is on the point of *striking in the face, with the heel of his hand, the opponent who is carrying the ball.* (See Rule XXIII., Sec. 1, Page 34.)

No. 30.

LEGAL TACKLING ABOVE THE KNEES—(See Rule XXIII., Sec. 8 (*b*), Page 36.)

Spalding's Official Football Guide. *The annual publication reported on changes made by the rules committee each year; it also reprinted Walter Camp's yearly All-America Team selections.*

William "Pudge" Heffelfinger (left) and Lee "Bum" McClung at the Yale fence, 1891. Heffelfinger was selected to Walter Camp's All-America Team in 1889, 1890, and 1891. McClung received the same honor in 1890 and 1891.

would go over to the Camp's house in New Haven for a review of strategy."

That 1888 team may have been Yale's greatest. They were unbeaten, untied, and unscored upon throughout a 13-game season. The team that featured such immortal stars as Heffelfinger and Amos Alonzo Stagg rolled up 698 points. "A parent is like a coach," Camp once said. "If he is a good one he teaches his boy to grow; if he is a poor one he only teaches him to remember." One of the good ones, Camp watched as Stagg later became a legendary coach in his own right.

Platoon-style football, the use of separate offensive and defensive units on the same team, is a relatively new wrinkle in the sport. Through all of the nineteenth century and most of the twentieth, if a man played end on offense, he played the same position on defense.

Of seven men on the line of scrimmage, first referred to as "rushers," one man naturally stood in the middle. He was called the "center." The two men protecting him on either side were called "guards."

The men on the far outside were called, simply enough, the "end rushers;" later they came to be called "ends." The players standing second from the end, or between an end and a guard, made more tackles than the men from any other position. So they were called "tacklers" and, later, just "tackles."

To understand the origin of the quarterback's name, one must consider his position in relation to the halves and fullback. Before the center snapped the ball, the fullback would set up as the deepest man in the backfield. In Camp's 1891 book *American Football*, he

(Above) *Walter Camp coaching W.F. Knox, 1907. Although Camp initially objected to the forward pass, he was one of the first coaches to perfect its use. In 1906 and 1907, the forward pass enabled Yale to remain undefeated.* **(Overleaf, pages 66-67)** *"A Day With the Yale Team" by Frederic Remington. A sculptor and painter, Remington played Yale football in 1893. Reputedly, he dipped his football jacket in slaughter-house blood to make it look more businesslike.*

refers to the fullback simply as the "back." Flanking the back, on either side of him but much closer to the scrimmage line, were the two halfbacks. They stood roughly halfway between the men on the line and the back of the backfield. And the quarterback awaited the snap from center while standing approximately one quarter of the distance from the center to the back.

The standardization of the seven-man offensive line occurred in 1894. Intending to discourage the "mass momentum play," the IFA required that seven offensive players must stand at the scrimmage line when the play commenced. They also effectively outlawed one form of the flying wedge by requiring that a kickoff travel ten yards before anyone, on either team, could pick it up. And they passed another rule meant to decrease injuries when they reduced the time of a half from 45 minutes to 35. Some players, at this time, were developing nose guards and ear guards. Their patchwork concoctions would be the preliminaries to the helmet.

In 1903 Camp penned an essay requesting a penalty for unnecessarily roughing the kicker and "the more equable division of penalties and the greater certainty of their infliction." Glenn S. "Pop" Warner's Carlisle Indians used the hidden ball trick, or "hunchback play," that year to score a touchdown against Harvard. Carlisle's Jimmie Johnson received the opening kickoff and slipped the ball up under teammate Charlie Dillon's shirt. Dillon ran uncontested for a touchdown. Inspired by the Carlisle ends' habit of wearing padded football appliqués on the front of their jerseys and confusing the defensive team as to the identity of the ball carrier, Camp suggested a penalty for "unsportsmanlike conduct."

Camp was no champion of professional football. For his own contributions to the game, he accepted not a penny of recompense. He smelled professionalism even in collegiate football, aware that "ringers" would play for pay at one school, skirt the classroom, and when found out, register at another school. These "tramp" athletes might play for 10 or 15 years. Football, like basketball and baseball, would fall victim in the twentieth century to the fixing of games. Camp foresaw this when he said, "A man who begins by selling his skill to a college may someday find himself selling an individual act in a particular contest—selling races, selling games."

Theodore Roosevelt's gusto is legendary. In spite of asthma, poor vision, and a heart murmur, he hunted bear and buffalo, boxed, and possessed a passion for physical fitness. When President McKinley was assassinated, Vice President Roosevelt learned of the news while mountain climbing in the Adirondacks. He held football in such high regard that he asked prospective cabinet members, before he hired them, whether or not they had played the game.

In a letter to Camp, President Roosevelt wrote:

> We were tending steadily in America to produce in our leisure and sedentary classes a type of man not much above the Bengali Baboon, and from this the athletic spirit has saved us. Of all the games I personally like football the best, and I would rather see my boys play it than see them play any other. I have no patience with the people who

declaim against it because it necessitates rough play and occasional injuries!

The century's first decade was a heady era for journalists. Muckraking writers had their innings with corporate and political corruption, with labor racketeering, and presently they needed a new icon to assail. College football seemed perfect. Journalists went after the most prestigious eastern schools.

Owing in part to its violent image, football had by now achieved tremendous popularity. Nevertheless, many journalists demanded that the game be outlawed. When New York writers witnessed a death in an NYU-Union College game in 1905, the fires of protest were fueled.

The following year the *Chicago Tribune* cited 73 deaths in games from the previous year among high school, college, and semi-professional football. The numbers were never verified.

Edwin G. Dexter of the University of Illinois had conducted a survey on football injuries and deaths in 1902 and found his initial suspicions about the game's violence to have been exaggerated. Using accident-insurance statistics, a report he published in *Educational Review* demonstrated that horseback riding and baseball were more dangerous. The muckrakers ignored him.

Football, most will admit, is a game whose metaphor is war. A game is a battle; a season is a campaign. The game's object is to move as far as possible into the opponent's territory; the opponent tries with physical restraint to prevent such progress. A campaign's ultimate victor often is the unit which suffers the fewest casualties. The men on the front line are said to fight

(Above) *"The Foot-ball of the Future" from* Harper's Weekly, *1879.* **(Facing)** *Yale vs. Princeton, 1909. After an 1888 Yale-Wesleyan game, the* New Haven News*'s tally of Yale injuries was stunning: "Wallace has an abscess on his lip. Stagg had his right eye and nose badly banged up.... Graves has a bad cut on the top of his head. Woodruff's leg is... badly used up.... Bull has a badly strained tendon." Despite these handicaps, Yale won.*

trench warfare. You invade with a blitz. You destroy with a bomb. Then generals call the shots from afar.

Camp didn't deny this, though his moves to limit the violence are well documented. He had chaired an investigating committee in 1893-94, which gathered data concerning the frequency of football injuries. In part he saw the game as an opportunity to screen off a few fields where men could clash for a couple of hours each Saturday. Those unable or unwilling to play could enjoy the game vicariously. Camp thought the metaphor preferable to the real item.

President Theodore Roosevelt set out to make football a cleaner game. In 1905 he summoned Yale athletic director Walter Camp and head coach John Owsley, Harvard coach Bill Reid and team physician Edward Nichols, and Princeton head coach Arthur Hildebrand and professor James B. Fine to a White House football conference. He demanded that football be made a gentleman's game, much as baseball, the nation's pastime, was somewhat erroneously regarded. No more punching and kicking of opponents. Once again, Camp found himself responsible for reforming football.

Though the meeting satisfied the President, academics the caliber of Columbia's Nicholas Murray Butler and Harvard's Charles Eliot (president of the school since 1869) still wanted the sport abolished. Harvard's Corporation Board voted to cancel the Yale game that year, despite the fact that President Roosevelt, himself a Harvard graduate, held eight tickets to the game. The Washington press considered an appearance at a football match to be beneath the dignity of the executive office.

In the Harvard-Penn game that year, a Penn player kicked Harvard's Barthol Parker in the groin, leaving the Crimson player rolling on the ground in agony. Soon as he could gather the strength, Parker climbed to his feet and threw a punch so hard that it at once broke the Penn lineman's jaw and Parker's own hand. As so often happens when fisticuffs break out on the sporting field, the referee saw Parker's offense but not the act that precipitated it. For 24 hours it seemed the Harvard-Penn match might be the last intercollegiate football game ever played.

The next day Harvard's Coach Reid was at the White House with President Roosevelt. The latter demanded to know what had happened. Reid, who had been at the game the previous day, explained the situation in detail, then asked, "What would you have done, Mr. President, if you had received such a kick?"

"Well, I believe that in the heat of battle, I would have done exactly what young Parker did," answered the commander in chief.

Football carried on. Harvard and Yale met that year, but not without incident. After a Yale kick, an Eli ran into a Crimson punt receiver who had signaled for a fair catch. Forthwith throughout the grandstand, members of the country's two most distinguished institutions of higher learning commenced throwing punches at one another. An anti-football leader on hand sent a message to Coach Reid on the Harvard sideline, demanding that the Crimson eleven remove itself from the field. Reid refused.

The following week, President Eliot of Harvard

While the rules committee imposed penalties to prevent injuries and violence, their rules were often ignored by players and referees. Pictured here is a flagrant violation of the "handling" rule in a practice session.

Walter Camp (with back to camera) and members of the Intercollegiate Football Rules Committee (IFRC). The IFRC's first rule established eligibility requirements to prevent "tramp" athletes from playing college football.

announced that his institution would not schedule a 1906 football season.

Roosevelt called another White House meeting after the season, again inviting representatives from Harvard, Yale, and Princeton, and told them, "Do not report back to me until you have a game that is acceptable to the entire nation. You must act in the public interest. This glorious sport must be freed from brutality and foul play. The future of the republic is dependent upon what you do. The character of future generations is in your hands."

Afterward, Camp released this statement to the press:

> At a meeting with the President of the United States, it was agreed that we consider an honorable obligation exists to carry out in *letter* and in *spirit* the rules of the game of football, relating to roughness, holding, and foul play, and the active coaches of our universities being present with us, pledge themselves to so regard it and to do their utmost to carry out that obligation.

New York University's Chancellor Henry M. MacCracken called for all IFA colleges to join a conference. Twenty-eight responded and, calling themselves The Football Conference Committee, met at NYU on December 24, 1905. Their leader was Army's Palmer E. Pierce. Pierce and Camp met subsequently and agreed to merge the Conference Committee with Camp's IFA Rules Committee. Thus was initiated the Intercollegiate Football Rules Committee (IFRC), later named the National Collegiate Athletic Association.

The IFRC's first rules change concerned eligibility. Tramp athletes would be a thing of the past. "College football can only be cleansed if eligibility is restricted to sophomores, juniors,and seniors, with special instructional teams for entering freshmen," Camp said. "Any man who changes schools must wait one year before becoming eligible for the varsity. The tramp athlete can only be controlled if his path is strewn with obstacles."

The IFRC decided to reduce the length of a half again, this time to 30 minutes. It also called for the expulsion of players for fighting or for "kneeing an opposing player."

Camp, who had come up with the idea of three downs to gain five yards, could see now where it made for a savage game. It led to "mass plays," in which 22 players moved along, foot by foot, almost at a standstill. It was time to open the action up, so he suggested a set of four downs to gain ten yards. Also, the forward pass was instituted as a legal play. Despite having himself thrown the game's first documented (albeit controversial) forward pass, Camp as a mature man initially disapproved of the play. Eventually he capitulated, however, seeing that the pass would open the game further, reduce the advantage of the heavier player, and increase the odds for the faster player. Football would become a game in which brains and speed might prevail over brawn.

Finally, the committee determined that each game would have an impartial referee, rather than one hired by either of the institutions involved in the game. The routine during the 1890s had been for each team to hire a referee, and an umpire would settle their arguments. The humorous side of this was that referees often were

Whiffenpoofs in front of Mory's before the Yale-Brown game, 1914. Great fans of Yale football, the Whiffenpoofs originated in the back chamber of Mory's, a private Yale club. The singing group takes its name from a fictional creature, which, when lured with food, emerges from its den squawking.

selected for their ability to debate rather than for their knowledge of football.

The rules committee designated more violent acts as fouls, and this time the referees assessed the penalties. Mass plays were abolished once and for all, as was all interlocked interference and all pushing and pulling of the ball carrier by members of his own team.

The game changed significantly and suddenly. As a consequence, not only fans but many of the players couldn't keep track of the rules. A temporary proliferation of penalties ensued, inspiring one poet to write:

> You can talk of your backs,
> And your runners in packs,
>   And your quarterback speedy and tall,
> But just the same,
> In this newfangled game
>   It's the referee carries the ball!

Initial confusion notwithstanding, penalties saved football. Never again was the game threatened.

In 1906 field goals and touchdowns each counted five points, though a conversion after the touchdown counted an extra point, and a safety counted two. In 1910 the field goal would drop to three points and, in 1912, the touchdown became six points—just as Camp had intended, and just as it remains today.

The forward pass finally flourished in 1913, when Notre Dame quarterback Gus Dorais and receiver Knute Rockne beat Army with it.

On November 21, 1914, to Camp's delight, the Yale Bowl opened. The mammoth new stadium with a seating capacity of 70,896 filled for that Saturday's

"Handsome Dan," the Yale mascot.

The Yale Bowl's first game: Yale vs. Harvard, November 21, 1914. About 70,000 people attended "The Game," as the annual Yale-Harvard contest was known. One spectator remarked, "This 'bowl' is one of the most impressive structures that has ever been erected on any athletic field, and those who have not seen it will be surprised at its magnitude."

Harvard-Yale game. Its unveiling was testament not only to football's popularity but to the presumption of its staying power. One doesn't quickly tear down a stadium of 70,896 seats. The era of giant arenas was born, and the Yale Bowl stands today.

When the National Football League (NFL) enjoyed its inaugural season in 1919 (at a cost of $25 a franchise), Camp disapproved. He had worked much of his life to reserve football for amateurs; he feared professionalism would lead to corruption. In spite of the ever-popular Jim Thorpe's participation, few took the professional league seriously before the year of Camp's death. When George Halas signed college star Red Grange in 1925 to play for Halas's Chicago Bears, the league achieved validation in the public's eyes.

What would Camp have thought of today's overtly corporate game? Of the massive protective padding and thick helmets that render one player virtually indistinguishable from another? Of television time-outs or offensive and defensive platoons? What would he have thought of the phenomenon called the Super Bowl and its elaborate ceremony, about the fact that many Americans hold Super Bowl Sunday more sacrosanct than Easter Sunday?

"Football is never stationary," Camp once noted. "It is always developing one way or the other and is the most interesting of all our sports from that standpoint." Change, he knew, would always be the norm. It was inevitable.

Football changes as much as it does because it is a game of innovation. One team wins by out-thinking rather than overwhelming its opponent. Just as weaponry changes from one war to the next, the game of football is nearly unrecognizable from one era to another.

Certainly, Camp would have disdained the red-shirting of high school players in Texas. No editorial writer in the land would have been as opposed to athletic scholarships. But Camp, with appropriate reservations, would have welcomed the mass popularity of American football.

Recently, British television began airing taped-delayed broadcasts of NFL games. That his creation has made the jump back across the Atlantic would have delighted the man who Americanized the British game of rugby.

Indisputably, Walter Camp is the father of American football. We must credit him for the game's most important early innovations (the scrimmage, downs and yards to be gained, the 11-man team) and some of its most important reforms (the modern scoring system, penalties for unsportsmanlike play). An outstanding player, he was an even better coach. Rival coaches sought his counsel, and it is no wonder. In the years that Camp was associated with Yale football as player, coach, and advisor, the team won more than 95 percent of its games.

Football has evolved from a campus pickup game without any rules into a major commercial product that entertains millions. Far more than anyone else, Camp is responsible for this evolution. Football became and remains the principal college game. For many, it is the most identifiable symbol of college life. As the father of American football, Camp is by extension the father of intercollegiate athletics.

Victory celebrations turned into major events as thousands of spectators showed support for their favorite team by rushing onto the field, sometimes setting fire to the goal posts.

Sailors at the U.S. Naval Operative Base in Hampton Roads, Virginia, 1919. As part of their daily training program, sailors performed the Daily Dozen.

A STATESMAN FOR SPORT

The June 28, 1914, assassination of Archduke Francis Ferdinand of Austria-Hungary at Sarajevo, Yugoslavia, and the subsequent outbreak of world war focused attention on Europe. While America claimed neutrality, the global conflict had a significant impact on Walter Camp from the start.

The New Haven Clock Company, now headed by Camp as president, was inundated with foreign orders for clocks. Unfortunately, once made, the finished clocks began backing up in the warehouse as space on Europe-bound cargo carriers became increasingly limited. Undaunted, a middle-aged Camp focused his energies on developing a way to fit more clocks into the same size package, alleviating the need for additional cargo space. The puzzle engaged his full attention until April 6, 1917, when newspaper headlines announced that the United States had declared war on Germany.

America's entry in World War I thrust Camp from the private sphere to the public sphere as he looked for ways to improve the fitness of American troops heading to the front lines of France. Camp was first alerted to the need for improved physical conditioning by a letter from a rear admiral of the U.S. Navy, who, Camp says, "was about to throw out all set-up exercises from his district as they either tired his men out so that they were for a time unfit for strenuous drill or that it taught them to slack because they saw the opportunities of avoiding the actual proper performance of the exercises."

At the same time, Camp began hearing reports of vast numbers of young men who were being rejected at recruiting offices due to poor health and physique. Fifty-

(Above) *Walter Camp demonstrating the "Grate," 1918. One of the Daily Dozen, the Grate, according to Camp, developed a muscular cap over the shoulder.* **(Overleaf, pages 82-83)** *Sailors playing with a "medicine ball" at a U.S. Navy training camp, World War I. As athletic director of military training activities, Camp advocated team sports.*

The Daily Dozen
10¢ a copy
FOR MEN AND WOMEN
by WALTER CAMP
Take a Tip From the Tiger
and Stay Young!
THE REYNOLDS PUBLISHING COMPANY, INC.
416 WEST 13TH ST., NEW YORK

In his last book, The Daily Dozen, *Camp shared his philosophy for good living: "Work all the big muscles of the body daily. Get all the air, sunshine, and play you have time for. Avoid anger, jealousy, and worry. Drink 7 or 8 glasses of water a day. Keep clean in body and mind."*

eight years old and in better shape than men less than half his age, Camp considered it his patriotic duty to remedy the situation.

Camp traveled to the Navy training station, and what he saw there confirmed the concerns expressed by the rear admiral.

> "At the first station I visited, . . . lads were in bed with sharp attacks of measles, or sitting around in the throes of mumps, chicken pox, and other children's diseases," he said. "The surgeons were keenly alert to prevent the spread of such diseases, but their efforts were largely negatived by the overtiring effect of the setting-up drill. My task was to devise a simple system of movements that would build resistance—not crush it."

To accomplish his goal, Camp began looking at exercises used by other cultures. "I found few that were in existence that were not for the most part devoted to development of muscle and largely the muscles of the arms and legs," he said. "I found parts of several that had some body work. When I went back to the Yogis of India, I found the first of the tension trunk exercises. In Danish systems some excellent ones." But none of these programs entirely satisfied him.

> "It was not until I followed the wild animal in a state of captivity that it struck me that he was really our best example in these days of intense confinement," Camp recalled. "If you go to the Bronx Zoo you will never see the animals, the tigers and the lions, standing

up on their hind legs and pushing their forepaws up and down or flexing them in the muscle building attempt. But you will see them daily and hourly stretching those big muscles. It is inherited instinct, and he does it a dozen times a day. So here was the suggestion to take the forms of body stretching exercises—then add to those only such as should give poise and carriage needed because our lives have too much stooping over books and papers, open up the cramped chests, and put enough muscle on the shoulder blades and on the shoulders themselves to make us efficient and give us muscular control. From this evolved almost of itself the so-called 'Daily Dozen.'"

The Daily Dozen comprised 12 exercises, less vigorous than those previously used by the Navy, but which enabled trainees to increase their strength. Camp believed that "over-developed biceps, startling pectoral muscles, and a great many times tremendously muscled legs," were a disadvantage. "The real essential is," he claimed, "the engine, the part under the hood as it were—lungs, heart, and trunk."

Camp's exercise regime proved so effective that in May 1917, he received a letter from Josephus Daniels, Secretary of the Navy, who asked if Camp would meet with him in the nation's capital to discuss another way that Camp could help the Navy.

The New Haven resident accepted Daniels's invitation. It led to Camp's appointment as chairman of the Athletic

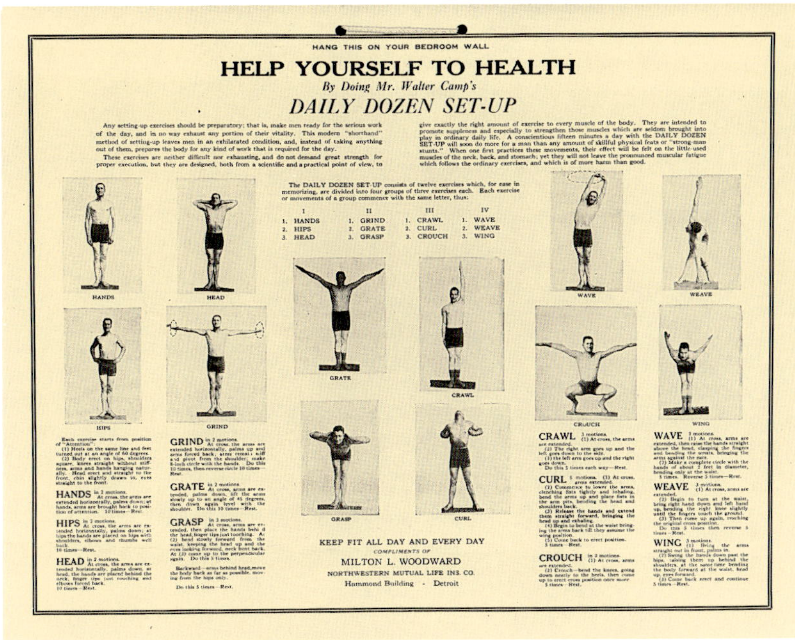

HANG THIS ON YOUR BEDROOM WALL

HELP YOURSELF TO HEALTH

By Doing Mr. Walter Camp's

DAILY DOZEN SET-UP

Any setting-up exercises should be preparatory; that is, make men ready for the serious work of the day, and in no way exhaust any portion of their vitality. This modern "shorthand" method of setting-up leaves men in an exhilarated condition, and, instead of taking anything out of them, prepares the body for any kind of work that is required for the day.

These exercises are neither difficult nor exhausting, and do not demand great strength for proper execution, but they are designed, both from a scientific and a practical point of view, to give exactly the right amount of exercise to every muscle of the body. They are intended to promote suppleness and especially to strengthen those muscles which are seldom brought into play in ordinary daily life. A conscientious fifteen minutes a day with the DAILY DOZEN SET-UP will soon do more for a man than any amount of skillful physical feats or "strong-man stunts." When one first practices these movements, their effect will be felt on the little-used muscles of the neck, back, and stomach; yet they will not leave the pronounced muscular fatigue which follows the ordinary exercises, and which is of more harm than good.

The DAILY DOZEN SET-UP consists of twelve exercises which, for ease in memorizing, are divided into four groups of three exercises each. Each exercise or movements of a group commence with the same letter, thus:

I	II	III	IV
1. HANDS	1. GRIND	1. CRAWL	1. WAVE
2. HIPS	2. GRATE	2. CURL	2. WEAVE
3. HEAD	3. GRASP	3. CROUCH	3. WING

HANDS HEAD WAVE WEAVE HIPS GRIND GRATE CRAWL CROUCH WING GRASP CURL

HANDS

HIPS

HEAD

GRIND

GRATE

GRASP

CRAWL

CURL

CROUCH

WAVE

WEAVE

WING

KEEP FIT ALL DAY AND EVERY DAY

COMPLIMENTS OF

MILTON L. WOODWARD

NORTHWESTERN MUTUAL LIFE INS. CO.

Hammond Building - Detroit

Walter Camp believed that the Daily Dozen would help less active, working adults achieve a higher level of fitness. Over time, newspapers, magazines, brochures, and phonograph records featured the popular exercise program.

Military personnel playing volleyball. Walter Camp said that he was "much opposed to any kind of work . . . which has not the element of fun in it."

Department of the U.S. Navy Commission on Training Camp Activities, a position that he held throughout the war. Shortly after meeting Daniels, Camp also became physical director for the U.S. Army Air Service.

"No branch of modern warfare is more delicate than that of Aviation," he said. "Man has only recently become a bird, and, removed from his normal conditions, he has much adjustment to make.... One of the cardinal requirements of the Aviator is suppleness and quick co-ordination of mind and muscle. Upon these depend not only his efficiency but his very life."

Besides introducing the 12 setting-up exercises to the military training camps, Camp also ensured that soldiers had ample opportunities to play team sports. There was a sentiment shared among military brass, including U.S. Army General John J. Pershing, that the military was similar to a football team. Both groups, it was agreed, used strict discipline to put men in tip-top physical condition, while at the same time, encouraging individual members of the group to take advantage of sudden opportunities to display brilliant physical action. Camp once said, "Men who play together and exercise together soon grow to know and understand each other." He, like Pershing and other top military personnel, knew that such camaraderie was the essence of the military, where men depended on each other for their lives.

Unfortunately, while Camp advanced team sports in U.S. training camps, many American colleges and universities made plans to abandon football until the war was over. The move came about, in part, because the young men with the most athletic ability were enlisting in the armed services, leaving few others to field college teams. In addition, some believed that it was unpatriotic for citizens to enjoy themselves at home while American soldiers laid their lives on the line overseas. Camp found the situation regrettable.

> "We hear some wails that the sport of football would be forgotten for the period of the war," he said. "Never was there a more foolish fear. Football IS war on a mimic scale and it will continue just as long as the nation is virile enough to fight.... When the commanders, either American or foreign, tell of the results of this sport upon the morale and fighting spirit of their men, they are only repeating what was evident at the very outbreak of the war in this country. The entire teams of our leading universities rushed to the colors. The 'gridiron warriors' as they had been called before we had a war doffed the moleskin and jersey for the khaki, stepped right off the lime-marked gridiron on to the parade ground, and they carried with them that fighting spirit for which our football men have been so justly celebrated. The same courage, patience, and persistence with which they had developed their football attack was needed in the drill and preparation for war. The same discipline, coordination, and quick thinking which was required on the football field was demanded in the corps. And best of all that grand do-or-die spirit that

The "Walter Scamps," 1917. U.S. government officials and cabinet members participated in an exercise program set up by Walter Camp during World War I. The eighth man from the left in the back row is Franklin D. Roosevelt, then Assistant Secretary of the Navy.

holds the attack on the one-yard line was
what made Château-Thierry."

Camp's efforts to improve American fitness were not confined to the military. Prompted by reports that European government leaders were collapsing from stress, he sought a way to prevent U.S. government leaders from sharing the same fate.

Camp felt that the United States could "ill afford to lose its most skilled Executives, both in the Government Departments and from among Manufacturing, Transportation, and Commercial interests, who are now from a sense of duty offering their services to the Government in this emergency." Sure that his Daily Dozen would benefit top-ranking government officials, Camp traveled to Washington, D.C., where he convinced members of President Woodrow Wilson's cabinet, plus others in federal service, to join a voluntary exercise program.

"Please don't think me a visionary," he wrote to William Cox Redfield, U.S. Secretary of Commerce, in an effort to gain his participation. "Although [the Daily Dozen] is not a new submarine or aeroplane, it is nevertheless a man saver."

The first meeting of the newly formed "Walter Scamps" occurred in the summer of 1917 in the yard behind the U.S. Treasury Building in Washington. Among those in attendance were Frank L. Polk from the State Department, Solicitor General John W. Davis, Attorney General Thomas N. Gregory, Secretary of the Interior Franklin K. Lane, Daniel C. Roper of the Tariff Commission, Paul Warburg of the Federal Reserve Board, Secretary of Labor William B. Wilson, Assistant Secretary

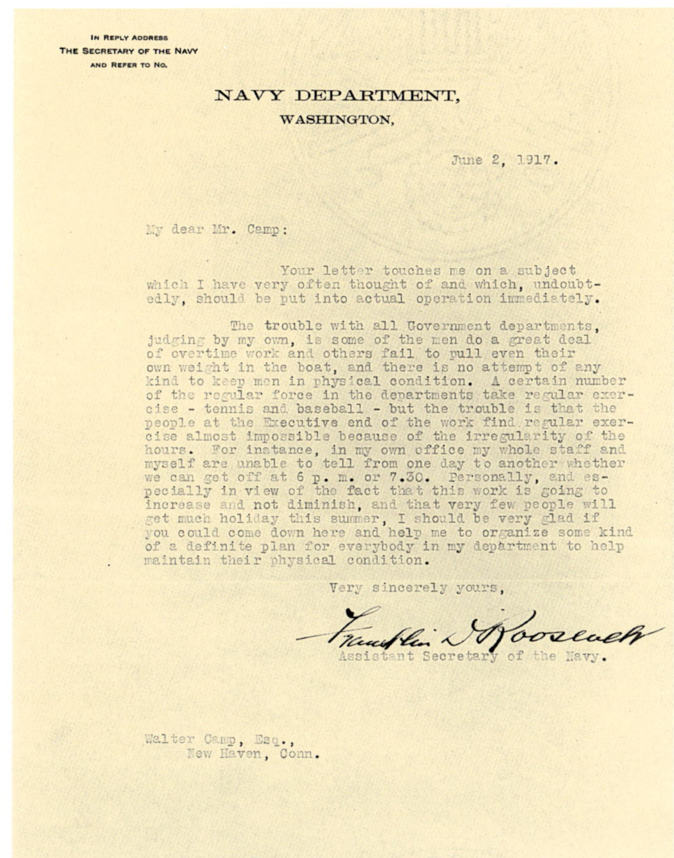

IN REPLY ADDRESS
THE SECRETARY OF THE NAVY
AND REFER TO NO.

NAVY DEPARTMENT,
WASHINGTON,

June 2, 1917.

My dear Mr. Camp:

Your letter touches me on a subject which I have very often thought of and which, undoubtedly, should be put into actual operation immediately.

The trouble with all Government departments, judging by my own, is some of the men do a great deal of overtime work and others fail to pull even their own weight in the boat, and there is no attempt of any kind to keep men in physical condition. A certain number of the regular force in the departments take regular exercise - tennis and baseball - but the trouble is that the people at the Executive end of the work find regular exercise almost impossible because of the irregularity of the hours. For instance, in my own office my whole staff and myself are unable to tell from one day to another whether we can get off at 6 p. m. or 7.30. Personally, and especially in view of the fact that this work is going to increase and not diminish, and that very few people will get much holiday this summer, I should be very glad if you could come down here and help me to organize some kind of a definite plan for everybody in my department to help maintain their physical condition.

Very sincerely yours,

Franklin D Roosevelt
Assistant Secretary of the Navy.

Walter Camp, Esq.,
New Haven, Conn.

Franklin D. Roosevelt, a believer in exercise, requested Walter Camp's assistance in creating a physical fitness program for himself and his staff.

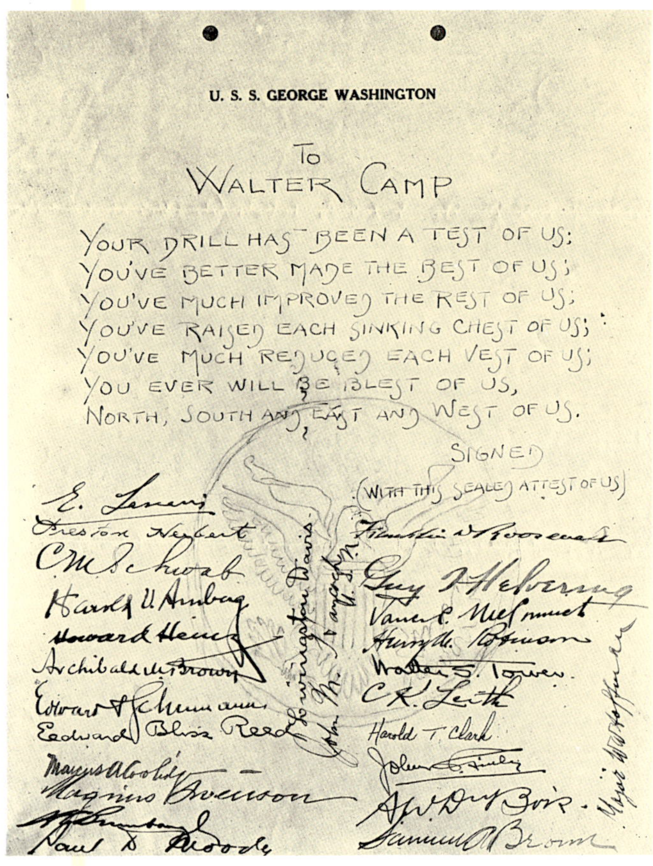

U. S. S. GEORGE WASHINGTON

TO

WALTER CAMP

YOUR DRILL HAS BEEN A TEST OF US;
YOU'VE BETTER MADE THE BEST OF US;
YOU'VE MUCH IMPROVED THE REST OF US;
YOU'VE RAISED EACH SINKING CHEST OF US;
YOU'VE MUCH REDUCED EACH VEST OF US;
YOU EVER WILL BE BLEST OF US,
NORTH, SOUTH AND, EAST AND WEST OF US.

SIGNED

(WITH THIS SEALED ATTEST OF US)

(Above) *A "thank you" from the "Walter Scamps."* **(Facing)** *Executive Committee, New Haven Senior Service Corps: (left to right) Isaac M. Ullman, president of the New Haven Chamber of Commerce; former U.S. President William H. Taft; and Walter Camp.* **(Overleaf, pages 92-93)** *Dr. W.C. Anderson demonstrates proper posture to the Senior Service Corps, which includes a suspendered William H. Taft.*

of Labor Louis F. Post, and Assistant Secretary of the Navy Franklin D. Roosevelt.

Besides instructing the Scamps in the proper execution of the Daily Dozen, Camp assessed each participant's present physical condition and recommended ways in which the individual could strengthen his body, as well as reduce stress during the course of the war. To all, he suggested a bath and a rubdown every morning before breakfast.

Later, en route to Brest, France, aboard the U.S.S. *George Washington,* the Scamps composed a poem to honor the man who had trained them. One of its authors, Franklin D. Roosevelt, later wrote to Camp, "I find that this job of running the Navy Department all alone means about fourteen hours a day if one is to do it well, but those exercises on the good ship *George Washington* have made the fourteen hours possible, and my only complaint is that I have gained ten pounds, luckily most of it in the right place."

The Walter Scamps weren't the only ones to benefit from Camp's training. In April 1917 Camp had established and organized the New Haven branch of the Senior Service Corps for men above military service age. William Howard Taft, who had joined the faculty of Yale College in New Haven after leaving the U.S. Presidency in 1913, was among the club's first members.

New branches of the Senior Service Corps quickly cropped up across the country, as citizens clamored for an opportunity to exhibit their patriotism at home. Members spent an hour a day, three times a week, exercising and marching.

11
10
8

"Riches do not make a race and machines alone will not win a war," Camp once exclaimed. "The issue always comes down to the fighting qualities of the people. Courage and stamina become the great asset, and neither is purchasable at a moment's notice. They must be in the Nation, lived in and cultivated." His belief in physical fitness for national preparedness became a battle cry shared by the American people.

Armistice was declared on November 11, 1918, at Compiègne, France, and Camp, no longer beset by official military obligations, decided to share his Daily Dozen program with the rest of the country. His greatest ambition, he confided to a colleague on the football rules committee, was to "make the nation fit." He believed that "all the art, literature, and education of the country may be at the mercy of a savage people unless the nation has enough real men who are ready to fight to preserve the things that a people value."

As if to confirm Camp's worst suspicions, end-of-war statistics proved that nearly half the men eligible for military service before the war began had been unable to enlist for reasons relating to health. Camp became further convinced that America's self-preservation depended on a healthier, fitter nation.

While Camp was deciding the best way to get the Daily Dozen into the hands of the public, several businessmen contacted him to see if he'd be interested in heading a fitness facility, to be named the Walter Camp Health Institute. Camp gave the idea serious consideration but declined the offer, thinking the institute would attract the middle-aged and out-of-shape rather than affect the attitudes of young Americans about exercise.

Instead, he accepted an offer by the editor of *American Magazine* to write an article describing the Daily Dozen in one of its upcoming issues. Once the magazine hit the newsstands, the Daily Dozen became an overnight success.

People everywhere sent letters to Camp, inviting him to demonstrate the exercise program at their homes, businesses, and clubs. One such invitation came from an association of credit men.

> "Naturally, this occupation is more or less sedentary, and must be so," Camp said after speaking at the association's convention. "For that reason, physical fitness for such men cannot depend merely upon a day a week of sports or games, although that helps greatly, but it must have a stronger backing in the form of a definite daily short period of stretching the unused muscles and keeping the circulation in proper condition. It is extraordinary how little time is required to do this. Less than ten minutes a day, if the work is systematically laid out, so that the greatest good is returned from the smallest expenditure of time. This is one of the reasons why the 'Daily Dozen' has been so largely adopted."

As the invitations became more and more numerous, Camp, who tried to accept when he could, found himself traveling with great frequency. Furthermore, each day's mail overflowed with letters asking him for favors or to clarify some point on the proper execution of the various exercises.

"Is it not more beneficial to the employees to omit the exercises on very hot days than to conduct the exercises in the boiling hot sun?" asked a store manager whose 100 employees exercised on the roof of the company's 18-story building.

"[We] would like to have your permission to have our artist make drawings of the [Daily Dozen] figures, using a scout as the subject," requested a Boy Scout leader.

Camp responded to each letter he received, but the demand on his time became so great that he approached *Collier's Weekly,* which already published his annual All-America Team, introduced in 1889, and which had recently affiliated with the publishers of *American Magazine*, to ask if they'd be interested in publishing an article that presented the Daily Dozen more fully. The idea appealed to the *Collier's* staff, and on August 5, 1920, the expanded Daily Dozen piece appeared.

To Camp's delight the *Collier's* issue sold out soon after it hit the stands. Thousands of requests for reprints arrived in the magazine's daily mail, so a brochure was created, and more than 400,000 of them were sold for a dime apiece.

The Daily Dozen swept the nation. Insurance company brochures, health magazines, business literature, newspaper articles, and phonographic records, all featured the now-famous exercise program. Camp also wrote two books on the Daily Dozen, one called *Keeping Fit All the Way*, published in 1919 by Harper and Row, and the other, *The Daily Dozen*, published by

Walter Camp, who wrote more than 250 articles for newspapers and magazines and upwards of 30 books, was one of the highest paid non-fiction writers of his day.

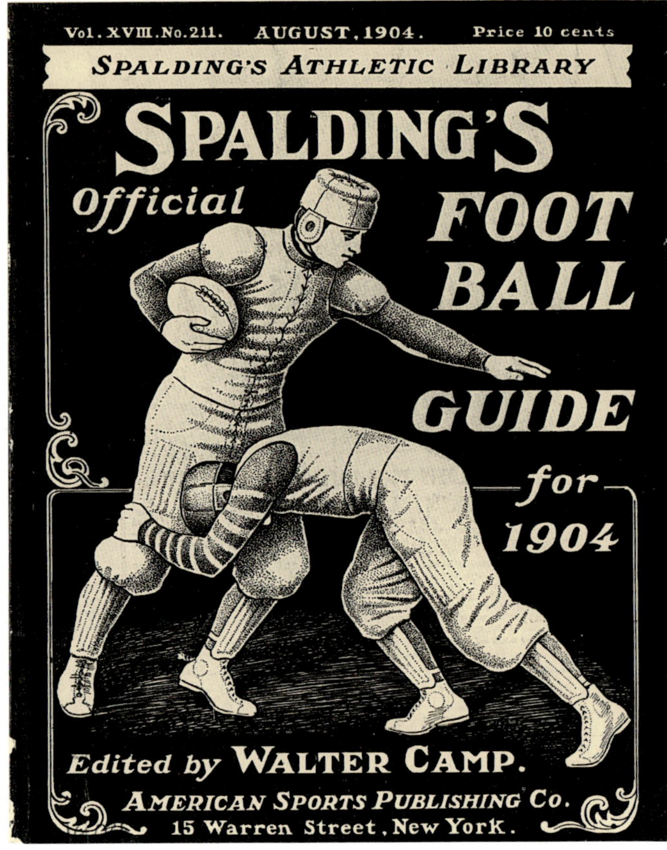

Spalding's Official Football Guide, *1904. Considered to be the foremost authority on football, Walter Camp edited the guide for many years.*

The Reynolds Publishing Company in 1925.

But Camp's popularity as a writer predated the Daily Dozen by some 30 years. His more than 250 articles, mostly on athletics and physical fitness, were published in a variety of popular magazines, including *Collier's Weekly, Harper's Weekly, Outing, Vanity Fair,* and *Youth's Companion*. He wrote for regional newspapers like the *Philadelphia Public Ledger,* as well as nationally as a syndicated columnist for the Consolidated Press Association beginning in 1922.

Additionally, Camp edited *Spalding's Official Football Guide* and *Boy's Magazine* and wrote more than 30 books. Only seven, including *The Substitute* and *Jack Hall at Yale,* were fictional. Not surprisingly, the heroes of these stories embodied many of the ideals that the author held most dear: honor, fair play, dedication, and sacrifice.

One of Camp's characters, Danny Phipps, possessed natural athletic abilities, but his talents were hampered on the gridiron by his quick temper. Danny "Fists," as his friends began to call him, became a star football player only after he learned self-control. "My belief," Camp once said, "is that it is the head and the heart and the willingness to work which count quite so much as the physical build."

Of Camp's non-fiction books, *American Football, The Book of College Sports,* and *Football Facts and Figures* were best known.

Camp loved writing adages. Always one to practice what he preached, he believed that "warm feet and a cool head will keep you clear of physicians" and that "nature made a mistake when she put a hard skull around a man's brain and failed to put an iron band around his abdomen."

The talented author wrote poetry. One poem, about the need for physical fitness for national preparedness, appeared on September 29, 1914, on the editorial page of the *New York American* and admonished, "Americans Awake!" Many of his poems dealt with sports, such as this untitled composition:

Oh center, fat and big,
How deadly dull you are!
You had the starting "sig"
Oh prithee! where's the ball?

The backs have started fast,
My hands extended are,
Oh center, they are past!
And prithee! where's the ball?

The other team's come through,
They've made our line a sieve,
And now at last from you—
Confound you! comes the ball!

During his writing career, Camp became one of the highest paid non-fiction writers in America. His articles touched a wide variety of subjects, from detailed commentaries on recent college football games, to advice for fighting the common cold, to entreaties for people to take fitness as seriously as they did religion.

"The gospel of exercise and of fresh air must be preached and practiced from the tiny tot playing in the newly found sand under the direction of the playground matron up to the old man who, although nearly fourscore, boasts of having had his full round of golf every Saturday at home and half the winter in the South," he firmly believed.

The secret to changing the public's perceptions about physical activity, Camp felt, was the "popularization of physical education, its introduction into the public schools and colleges," and "the operation of public playgrounds."

He encouraged Americans to use memorial gifts for building athletic fields, clubs, and playgrounds. "There is no practical value in an arch or a monolith," he said. "True, they perpetuate the memory of the occasion, but when we can combine the two and make something of distinct practical value and use, there ought to be no question in our minds."

A number of Camp's articles counseled businessmen to avoid succumbing to stress and one's emotions. In "Rattlesnakes" Camp wrote:

> Anger, jealousy, and fear are just as deadly to you as the rattlesnake. If the poisons of these three get into your blood they will ruin your health and your happiness and absolutely wreck your whole life. You must make yourself immune to these poisons. You can do it by exercise of mind and body. Strength of body and health brace up the mental processes so that those snakes cannot strike effectively.

Vacations were another thing Camp championed. In "The Squeezed Orange," Camp wrote:

> One of the most fatal things that can happen to any man no matter what his position in life is to become so tied up in his job that he does nothing else. It is appalling how rapidly all his juice of life is squeezed out of him until nothing is left but skin and pulp. And the worst of all is that there is no reward for any such devotion to this job for when his orange is sufficiently squeezed it is cast aside and nobody misses it. Everyone must have something to think about at times outside the deadly monotony of ceaseless grind.... Work does not kill. Worry and monotony do.

As a preventative, Camp suggested that people take an annual vacation of three successive weeks. Only a long period of time, he felt, was sufficient to clear one's mind of business-related matters and permit total relaxation.

Furthermore, holidays were to be kept simple. "Strange as it may seem, a great many people get more enjoyment out of anticipating the holiday season than from the reality," he said. "If the vacation doesn't live up to the prospect, it is because you do not know how to make the most of it; and making the most of a vacation consists very often in not making too much of it."

To Camp, a healthy body and mind were as important to attaining success in the business world as hard work. "Nemesis may be lame," he once claimed, "but in the long run she always catches the man that goes without exercise. Moreover, such a man is not prepared for the test when it comes."

The best training for a business career, Camp said, was a year or two on the college gridiron, although "its preparation for life work has never received its proper consideration. There is no sport which is so highly organized or which bears such a striking similarity to our complex business organization as this fall game."

As evidence, Camp cited the rise of football jargon in corporate communications: "team work," "hitting the line," "method of attack," and "playing the game" were among the phrases he noted.

> "The reason that all these football terms have been incorporated into the language of business is they furnish such forcible illustrations that not only the man who makes a specialty of efficiency uses them," he said, "but it is also true that every able executive drops into the language of the gridiron when he wishes, to especially emphasize force, rigor, and drive. It is because our American game of football has become the most specialized school for the inculcation of these attributes under a network of organization comparable only to that of our most successful and broadly extended business or financial institutions."

Camp's intellectual and emotional passion for the game of American football was unparalalled. Over the years, he corresponded with thousands of individuals on the topic. He followed college football around the country as if his life depended on it. His keen mind and brilliant powers of observation enabled him to analyze plays and, with great foresight, predict how the game needed to evolve. When debate arose over the intent of a rule or the clarification of a penalty, people turned to Camp as the final arbiter. His intense love for the game was matched only by his eloquence:

"When the football season comes there begins to stir, at first mildly, then with more and more force, and finally with actual violence, the desire to see the very pick and flower of the youth of the land contend in this game that combines brains and brawn, strategy and strength, as probably no other contest yet devised."

Camp's last book, *The Daily Dozen*, is considered the most revealing. More than an exercise book, it outlines the very philosophies for healthy living by which Camp himself lived his life.

In *The Daily Dozen* Camp wrote:

> There are two kinds of men in the world today.... One kind, when they want anything, sit down and hope for it. The other kind pull up their belts a hole tighter and go out after it.
>
> No man can wander along, wishing half-heartedly that he drank and smoked less and that he kept himself in better physical trim, and then expect to be transformed painlessly into another kind of individual with purpose and perseverance and pluck enough to keep fit. The only way to cut down on cigarettes is to cut down. The only way to refuse to let yourself get puffy and short-winded and red-eyed from too many cocktails is to refuse those cocktails. The way to stop is to stop.
>
> Any victory in life is worth everything it costs if it comes through determination, the use of brains, discipline, and self-denial.

To Camp, success resulted from total commitment. Hard work wasn't the key; hard and *continued* work was. He believed that the only things that ever came quickly in life were disappointments.

On Friday, March 13, 1925, Camp left New Haven for a meeting of the football rules committee that was being held in New York City. It would be his last trip. In the early morning hours of the 14th, Camp died in his sleep, the victim of a heart attack. When he failed to appear Saturday morning for the meeting, William W. Roper, Princeton's football coach, and W.S. Langford of Trinity College went to his room, where they found his lifeless body in peaceful repose. Given that football was the greatest passion of this extraordinary man's rich and varied life, it was as if the custodian of the game had picked his place to die.

News of Camp's death traveled quickly, and the widowed Alice received thousands of letters and telegrams from friends, family, and fans offering her their condolences. Nearly every newspaper in America paid editorial tribute to the legendary man.

On March 16, 200 mourners attended a simple 20-minute service for Walter at the Camp's Humphrey Street home. The service was followed by a graveside ceremony, led by the Reverend Roy M. Houghton, pastor of the Church of the Redeemer, at Evergreen Cemetery.

Under cloudless skies, the father of American football and the hero of a nation was laid to rest.

The 1889 Yale Varsity Football Team.
Captain C.O. Gill holds the ball.

THE LEGACY OF WALTER CAMP

Walter Camp named his first All-America Team in 1889. Only football players from three colleges—Yale, Harvard, and Princeton—made the 1889 team: Amos Alonzo Stagg, William "Pudge" Heffelfinger, Edgar Allan Poe (grandnephew and namesake of the renowned writer), Arthur Cummock, Hector W. Cowan, John Cranston, William J. George, Charles O. Gill, James T. Lee, Roscoe H. Channing Jr., and Knowlton Ames.

By today's standards, limiting such an award to only three colleges, and Ivy League schools at that, seems overtly biased. But back in 1889, American college football was in its infancy, and few colleges had teams, let alone sterling players. Over time the sport's popularity spread, and football became part of the athletic program of colleges across the country.

In the early years of the All-America Team, Ivy Leagues dominated the roster. The Big Three were joined by other Ivy League schools, when in 1891 the University of Pennsylvania and, a few years later, Cornell saw their players make the team.

By 1899 the quality of football being played outside of the Ivy League inspired Camp to select Isaac Seneca of the Carlisle Indian Institute to the All-America Team. As football's popularity spread, the composition of the annual team continued to change until, in 1924, players for Harvard, Yale, and Princeton were for the first time conspicuously absent.

Camp's hand-picked All-America Teams remain unique, for they comprised 11 men best suited to fill the various positions on a football *team*, as opposed to simply the 11 best American football players. The

Princeton's Edgar Allan Poe (left) and a teammate. Poe, nicknamed "The Little Wonder," played left end and was the Princeton Tigers' captain in 1889.

Princeton's 1889 Varsity Football Team. In 1889 the Tigers were the league champions.

Harvard's 1888 Varsity Football Team.

Harvard tackle Marshall Newell, a Walter Camp All-American in 1891, 1892, and 1893.

distinction, while subtle, separated Camp's All-Americans from newer consensus teams that began appearing in publications across the nation, as well as subsequent All-Americans selected after Camp's death.

The All-Eastern Team, All-Western Team, and All-Scholastic Team were just three of the imitators being offered to the American public. By 1908 the team fad had reached its height, when 36 different teams appeared in newspapers around the country. Asked his opinion on one such consensus team, Camp commented, "Those are eleven good men, but the captain will be sorry to find out, in the game, that he has nobody who can kick the ball."

Of course, as the popularity of college football spread across the country, the task of narrowing down a nation full of talented football players to a squad of 11 proved difficult. As a result, Camp relied on reports by trusted colleagues and correspondents, who contacted him with information about the abilities of players in their regions.

From their recommendations, Camp compiled a list of about 100 gifted players at the start of each football season. As the weeks progressed, additional reports filtered in from the field, and Camp himself traveled all over the country in order to watch the nation's best football players perform on the gridiron. By season's end, Camp had pared the 100 until 11 remained.

Few players made Camp's team more than once, and only a handful were selected by Camp all four years that they played college football: Harvard's Marshall Newell, University of Pennsylvania's T. Truxton Hare, and Yale's Frank A. Hinkey and Gordon Brown. None of these athletes was selected based on his performance in the previous season. The only thing that mattered to Camp was demonstrated ability on the football field for the current year.

It wasn't long before Camp's All-America Team became so popular that the sports pages of newspapers coast to coast ran the list after the year's players had been announced in a fall edition of *Collier's Weekly*. Editors from other magazines tried to woo Camp and his All-America selections away from the popular magazine, but without success.

One year a thief broke into the *Collier's* printer, stole the list, and tried to sell it to another publication. To prevent future thefts, Camp began splitting the team into three groups and submitting the sections to *Collier's* under separate cover. Only at press time was the team "reunited."

For 25 years Camp and the All-America Team were synomymous. Harold "Red" Grange, the University of Illinois' "Galloping Ghost," remarked that "Camp was the No. 1 name in football; if you weren't on the Camp team, it didn't mean a thing."

When Camp's death in 1925 left *Collier's Weekly* with a hole in its editorial calendar, the editors turned to another famous sports writer, Grantland Rice, and asked him to take over the All-America Team selections. Rice agreed, but not before receiving permission to pay tribute to his predecessor in a article that appeared in the May 9, 1925, issue of *Collier's*. In it Rice wrote:

> [The All-America Team] was a great idea, and what is still more important, it was

handled by the right man.... In addition to his inside knowledge of the playing and the coaching end, Walter Camp brought to his selection of the annual All-America football team...keen judgment without bias or prejudice, a broad national viewpoint, and the friendly assistance of the leading coaches from coast to coast.... There was nothing hit-or-miss about it, no guessing, no intrusion of personal likes or dislikes. It was a stupendous undertaking.

Unlike Camp before him, Rice based his All-America choices on a consensus vote. He continued the annual selection until his death in 1948; afterwards, the team was selected by consensus through wire services, sports editors, and others over the years.

With his uncanny aptitude for predicting the future of athletics and physical fitness in America, Camp developed a loyal and devoted following of fans, spanning the spectrum of ages and backgrounds. Young children adored him. Football players stood in awe of him. Business adversaries respected him. And when he died, a nation mourned him.

Many post-mortem tributes were paid to Camp. The trustees of Hopkins Grammar School acknowledged his grievous loss in their minutes. On October 23, 1926, Harvard and Dartmouth dedicated their football game "to the memory of Walter Camp in recognition of his enduring service to American Football and his life work for clean sport as a tremendous influence on the physical and moral health of the world." Newspapers like *The New York Times* declared him the "prophet" of the "Age

(Above) *Frank A. Hinkey, Yale end from 1891 to 1894. Walter Camp selected Hinkey for the All-America Team each of the player's four years at Yale.* **(Facing)** *Yale alumni players gather for the 1901 Bicentennial Celebration game with the varsity team. The reunion gathering included Walter Camp (center with ball), William "Pudge" Heffelfinger, Lee "Bum" McClung, Pa Corbin, and Frank Butterworth.*

Bicentennial

(Above and facing) *Following Camp's death in 1925, many tributes were paid to him. The Walter Camp Memorial Gateway, built amid the Yale athletic fields in front of the Yale Bowl, bears 503 small bronze plaques, each with the name of a university or preparatory school that contributed money toward the memorial.*

of Athletics." Coaches such as Notre Dame's Knute Rockne acknowledged that "his loss to the sporting world will be irreparable."

But perhaps the biggest tribute to Camp occurred on November 3, 1928, when the Walter Camp Memorial Gateway was dedicated during the Yale-Dartmouth football game. Built at the entrance to the Yale playing fields, the massive gateway bears the simple inscription:

> Given by American Colleges and Schools to Honor Walter Camp and the Traditions of American College Sport Which He Exemplified.

Funds for the $300,000 memorial, designed by Yale alumnus John W. Cross, came from Yale alumni, as well as from the National Collegiate Athletic Association, which collected donations from 224 colleges and universities and 279 preparatory and high schools across America. Individual bronze plaques found on the memorial acknowledge each institution's contribution. More than anything else before it, the Walter Camp Memorial Gateway demonstrated the love that all Americans felt for the man who had popularized exercise and who had transformed English rugby into an American passion.

As a tribute to his unique innovations, Walter Camp was inducted into the National Football Foundation and Hall of Fame on November 3, 1951.

After that time, little attention was given to the memory of Walter Camp until, in 1967, a group of men from the New Haven, Connecticut, region gathered for dinner at a local restaurant and decided to honor the

Y.A. Tittle, former quarterback for the San Francisco Forty-Niners and the New York Giants, received the 1988 Walter Camp Distinguished American award.

father of American football by forming the Walter Camp Football Foundation. One of the first things that the charter members agreed to do was resurrect the Walter Camp All-America Team and return it to the stature it had enjoyed under Camp's guidance. In the years since then, their efforts have been highly successful.

The foundation's original mission, to encourage a better understanding of the benefits derived from participating in football and to perpetuate the ideals of Walter Camp through all levels of competition, has grown to include the support of a variety of charitable and worthwhile organizations, ranging from the Connecticut Special Olympics and Easter Seal's Low Vision Clinic to the Leukemia Society and the Save the Children Program. To date, the foundation's contributions total more than $350,000 to nearly 50 different organizations.

Each year the Walter Camp Foundation surveys coaches and sports information directors from colleges and universities throughout the nation to get their nominations for each position on the All-America Team, as well as for Player of the Year and Coach of the Year. The athletes with the most votes per position or award are selected. Only ties are broken by foundation members. The selections are announced on Thanksgiving weekend.

No longer confined to just 11 men, as in Camp's time, today's All-America Team comprises 24 players, 12 on offense, including a place kicker, and 12 on defense, including a punter. The move to the 24-man team shows just how sophisticated the college sport has grown in the years since Camp played

To Camp's way of thinking, it wasn't enough to be a great athlete. One needed also to be a great human, and that included being a success at one's chosen profession. It also meant becoming actively involved in community service.

In keeping with the Walter Camp spirit, the foundation also pays annual tribute to outstanding Americans.

Since it was first bestowed in 1967, the Coach of the Year award has been given to the college football coach best able to inspire players to brilliant team performances on the gridiron while instilling in them a respect for sportsmanship and fair play.

The Walter Camp Man of the Year award goes to an individual who is closely associated with football as either a player, coach, or in a position that is closely attendant to the game. Additionally, he must be a recognized leader in his chosen profession and in his community.

Player of the Year honors fall to the college athlete who best demonstrates self-discipline, unselfish team play, a desire to excel, mature judgement, and leadership. He must exhibit "pluck," a phrase Camp often employed to describe a talented athlete, both on the field and off, where his performance must include a strong effort to better the lives of others.

More recent Walter Camp Foundation awards include a Distinguished American Award, first presented in 1978, which is given to the individual who best exemplifies the ideals of cooperation, teamwork, self-denial, honesty, integrity, dedication, and leadership. A Distinguished American need not have participated in football but must have attained success in a business or profession.

The newest foundation award goes to the Alumnus of the Year, an All-American who has distinguished himself off the playing field, either in his personal career or by community service, while maintaining good moral conduct and taking pride in having once been a Walter Camp All-American.

All-Americans and individual award winners are honored in late January or early February at a three-day extravaganza in New Haven hosted by the Walter Camp Foundation. Called the Walter Camp Weekend, the annual event has become one of the most prestigious and successful in the nation.

One of the weekend's primary goals is to emphasize to the new All-Americans the value of community service. The foundation wants to ensure that when young athletes are selected to the team, they don't see the honor as just another trophy. Rather, foundation members reinforce the notion that the players really are part of a team, one that includes yesterday's legends and tomorrow's stars, all working together off the gridiron to better the lives of those around them. They hope to instill in newly appointed All-Americans the same code of honor and ethics and the same desire to excel that Camp stressed to the athletes of his day.

From the start of the Walter Camp Weekend, new All-Americans find themselves being made a part of the New Haven community. On Thursday evening the young athletes join their predecessors, many of whom are now All-National Football League players, for a novelty-style

81

75
72

(Above) *Dan Marino, a 1981 Walter Camp All-American, assists children competing in the Special Olympics.* (Overleaf, pages 112-113) *A former end for the New York Giants, Andy Robustelli (#81) became the Walter Camp Man of the Year in 1988.*

basketball game at a local sporting facility. Between 3,000 and 5,000 people from Connecticut come to watch, and proceeds from the event, as well as those collected at other functions during the weekend, benefit the various charities that the foundation supports.

The following morning after breakfast, the All-Americans are divided into groups and travel to the children's wards of the Yale-New Haven, St. Raphael, and Newington Children hospitals. During their visit, the football stars give the children souvenirs in the form of autographed photographs or small footballs.

That evening the All-Americans split up and, escorted by a foundation member and his family, have a one-on-one dinner at various New Haven restaurants. Besides giving New Haven residents a chance to see an All-American at one of several local eateries, the intimate dinner also gives every person in the all-volunteer foundation, as well as the award winners, a chance to get to know each other better. Other Walter Camp Foundation award winners eat at historic Mory's, a private club that has been a Yale tradition ever since college students en route from races on the harbor discovered its predecessor, Moriarty's ale house, in 1863. After dinner, the groups reunite at a local hotel for a social that is open to the public.

Saturday morning the press gets an opportunity to talk to the All-Americans over breakfast. Then, those award winners who do not own tuxedos (and most of the college-age All-Americans do not) must be fitted with formal outfits for the gala being held that evening.

A luncheon is held Saturday afternoon, where school-age New Haven youngsters and their parents dine at tables headed by All-Americans. Later the kids have a chance to have their pictures taken with the football stars.

The undisputed highlight of the Walter Camp Weekend takes place on Saturday night, when a formal reception followed by an elaborate black-tie awards banquet takes place at the Yale University Commons. Built at the turn of the century, the commons was selected as the site of the annual event not just for its elegant appearance and festive atmosphere but also because it conveys the sense of tradition and history unique to Yale College and, by association, Walter Camp.

More than 1,000 foundation members and guests gather to watch the presentation of the All-America Team, as well as the awarding of Player of the Year, Coach of the Year, Distinguished American, Man of the Year, and Alumnus of the Year honors. The event is presided over by Camp himself, whose calm countenance peers out over the room from a beautiful oil painting that hangs on one of the ornate wooden walls.

Were his presence at the dinner physical rather than spiritual, Walter Camp would be pleased to see his legacy—former All-Americans, distinguished citizens, all upholding the values he held most dear and coming together to honor and share their accomplishments.

As his colleagues on the Intercollegiate Football Rules Committee said in their memorial resolution to Camp in 1925: "American Rugby Football has lost its founder and its greatest champion, but his influence on the game will endure as long as the game is played."

The Walter Camp Football Foundation's annual awards dinner, Yale University Commons.

"Walter Camp"

Father of Football, Son of Fame,
In homage due, we may not fail;
Since you were one who played the game
For God, for Country, and for Yale.

You were a foeman Princeton feared,
An adversary Harvard knew,
And all the heirs of Eli cheered
Your exploits, when you wore the Blue.

But, ever loyal to your own,
You wished no rival lasting ill
And, widely as the sport has grown,
You had a vision wider still.

The code you fostered plays its part:
The code by which a boy may fight
In such a manner that his heart
Is ever high, his honor bright.

For you a distant trumpet pealed;
To pierce the mist our eyes are vain.
Who knows? Upon some fairer field
Perhaps you play the game again.

Naught but a promise can we give:
Oh, Walter Camp, as years sweep by,
While sportsmanship and football live,
Yours is a name which shall not die.

—Walter Trumbull

APPENDIX

Yale varsity player John Hunsicker (#75) leads team captain Phil Tarasovic (#74), trainer Dan Casman (in overcoat), and others off the field, 1955. This "modern" Yale team demonstrates just how much has changed since Walter Camp's first game in 1876. Among other things, rules calling for pads and helmets to protect players have redefined football's "look."

WALTER CAMP ALL-AMERICA TEAMS

1889
Arthur Cummock, *Harvard*
Hector W. Cowan, *Princeton*
John Cranston, *Harvard*
William J. George, *Princeton*
William W. Heffelfinger, *Yale*
Charles O. Gill, *Yale*
Amos Alonzo Stagg, *Yale*
Edgar Allan Poe, *Princeton*
James T. Lee, *Harvard*
Roscoe H. Channing Jr., *Princeton*
Knowlton Ames, *Princeton*

1890
Frank W. Hallowell, *Harvard*
Marshall Newell, *Harvard*
Jesse B. Riggs, *Princeton*
John Cranston, *Harvard*
William W. Heffelfinger, *Yale*
William C. Rhodes, *Yale*
Ralph H. Warren, *Princeton*
Dudley Dean, *Harvard*
John Corbett, *Harvard*
Lee McClung, *Yale*
Sheppard Homans Jr., *Princeton*

1891
Frank A. Hinkey, *Yale*
Wallace C. Winter, *Yale*
William W. Heffelfinger, *Yale*
John W. Adams, *Pennsylvania*
Jesse B. Riggs, *Princeton*
Marshall Newell, *Harvard*
John A. Hartwell, *Yale*
Phillip King, *Princeton*
Everett J. Lake, *Harvard*
Lee McClung, *Yale*
Sheppard Homans Jr., *Princeton*

1892
Frank A. Hinkey, *Yale*
A. Hamilton Wallis, *Yale*
Bert Waters, *Harvard*
William H. Lewis, *Harvard*
Arthur L. Wheeler, *Princeton*
Marshall Newell, *Harvard*
Frank W. Hallowell, *Harvard*
Vance McCormick, *Yale*
Charles Brewer, *Harvard*
Phillip King, *Princeton*
Harry C. Thayer, *Pennsylvania*

1893
Frank A. Hinkey, *Yale*
Langdon Lea, *Princeton*
Arthur L. Wheeler, *Princeton*
William H. Lewis, *Harvard*
William O. Hickock III, *Yale*
Marshall Newell, *Harvard*
Thomas S. Trenchard, *Princeton*
Phillip King, *Princeton*
Charles Brewer, *Harvard*
Franklin B. Morse, *Princeton*
Frank S. Butterworth, *Yale*

1894
Frank A. Hinkey, *Yale*
Bert Waters, *Harvard*
Arthur L. Wheeler, *Princeton*
Phillip T. Stillman, *Yale*
William O. Hickock III, *Yale*
Langdon Lea, *Princeton*
Charles Gelbert, *Pennsylvania*
George T. Adee, *Yale*
Arthur Knipe, *Pennsylvania*
George H. Brooke, *Pennsylvania*
Frank S. Butterworth, *Yale*

1895
Norman Cabot, *Harvard*
Langdon Lea, *Princeton*
Charles M. Wharton, *Pennsylvania*
Al Bull, *Pennsylvania*
Dudley Riggs, *Princeton*
Fred T. Murphy, *Yale*
Charles Gelbert, *Pennsylvania*
Clinton R. Wyckoff, *Cornell*
S. Brinckerhoff Thorne, *Yale*
Charles Brewer, *Harvard*
George H. Brooke, *Pennsylvania*

1896
Norman Cabot, *Harvard*
William W. Church, *Princeton*
Charles M. Wharton, *Pennsylvania*
Robert R. Gailey, *Princeton*
Wiley Woodruff, *Pennsylvania*
Fred T. Murphy, *Yale*
Charles Gelbert, *Pennsylvania*
William M. Fincke, *Yale*
Edgar N. Wrightington, *Harvard*
Addison W. Kelly, *Princeton*
John Baird, *Princeton*

1897
Garrett Cochran, *Princeton*
Burr C. Chamberlain, *Yale*
T. Truxton Hare, *Pennsylvania*
Alan E. Douchette, *Harvard*
Gordon Brown, *Yale*
John Outland, *Pennsylvania*
John A. Hall, *Yale*
Charles A. H. Desaulles, *Yale*
Benjamin H. Dibblee, *Harvard*
Addison W. Kelly, *Princeton*
John Minds, *Pennsylvania*

1898
Lew R. Palmer, *Princeton*
A. R. T. Hillebrand, *Princeton*
T. Truxton Hare, *Pennsylvania*
Peter Overfield, *Pennsylvania*
Gordon Brown, *Yale*
Burr C. Chamberlain, *Yale*
John W. Hallowell, *Harvard*
Charles D. Daly, *Harvard*
John Outland, *Pennsylvania*
Benjamin H. Dibblee, *Harvard*
Clarence B. Herschberger, *Chicago*

1899
David C. Campbell, *Harvard*
A. R. T. Hillebrand, *Princeton*
T. Truxton Hare, *Pennsylvania*
Peter Overfield, *Pennsylvania*
Gordon Brown, *Yale*
George S. Stillman, *Yale*
Arthur Pie, *Princeton*
Charles D. Daly, *Harvard*
Isaac Seneca, *Carlisle*
Josiah H. McCracken, *Pennsylvania*
Malcolm L. McBride, *Yale*

1900
David C. Campbell, *Harvard*
James R. Bloomer, *Yale*
Gordon Brown, *Yale*
Herman P. Olcott, *Yale*
T. Truxton Hare, *Pennsylvania*
George S. Stillman, *Yale*
John W. Hallowell, *Harvard*
William M. Fincke, *Yale*
George B. Chadwick, *Yale*
William Morley, *Columbia*
Perry T.W. Hale, *Yale*

1901 David C. Campbell, *Harvard*
Oliver F. Cutts, *Harvard*
William J. Warner, *Cornell*
Henry C. Holt, *Yale*
William G. Lee, *Harvard*
Paul B. Bunker, *Army*
Ralph T. Davis, *Princeton*
Charles G. Daly, *Army*
Robert P. Kernan, *Harvard*
Harold Weekes, *Columbia*
Thomas H. Graydon, *Harvard*

1902 Thomas L. Shevlin, *Yale*
James J. Hogan, *Yale*
John R. DeWitt, *Princeton*
Henry C. Holt, *Yale*
Edgar T. Glass, *Yale*
Gilbert Kinney, *Yale*
Edward Bowditch, *Harvard*
Foster Rockwell, *Yale*
George B. Chadwick, *Yale*
Paul B. Bunker, *Army*
Thomas H. Graydon, *Harvard*

1903 Howard H. Henry, *Princeton*
James J. Hogan, *Yale*
John R. DeWitt, *Princeton*
H. J. Hooper, *Dartmouth*
Andrew Marshall, *Harvard*
Daniel W. Knowlton, *Harvard*
Charles D. Rafferty, *Yale*
James E. Johnson, *Carlisle*
William Heston, *Michigan*
J. Dana Kafer, *Princeton*
Richard Smith, *Columbia*

1904 Thomas L. Shevlin, *Yale*
James L. Cooney, *Princeton*
Frank Piekarski, *Pennsylvania*
Arthur C. Tipton, *Army*
Gilbert Kinney, *Yale*
James J. Hogan, *Yale*
Walter H. Eckersall, *Chicago*
Vincent Stevenson, *Pennsylvania*
Daniel J. Hurley, *Harvard*
William Heston, *Michigan*
Andrew L. Smith, *Pennsylvania*

1905 Thomas L. Shevlin, *Yale*
Otis Lamson, *Pennsylvania*
Roswell C. Tripp, *Yale*
Robert Torrey, *Pennsylvania*
Francis H. Burr, *Harvard*
Beaton H. Squires, *Harvard*
Ralph Glaze, *Dartmouth*
Walter E. Eckersall, *Chicago*
Howard Roome, *Yale*
John H. Hubbard, *Amherst*
James B. McCormick, *Princeton*

1906 Robert W. Forbes, *Yale*
Horatio Biglow, *Yale*
Francis H. Burr, *Harvard*
W. T. Dunn, *Penn State*
Elmer Ives Thompson, *Cornell*
James L. Cooney, *Princeton*
L. Carpar Wister, *Princeton*
Walter H. Eckersall, *Chicago*
John W. Hayhew, *Brown*
William F. Knox, *Yale*
Paul L. Veeder, *Yale*

1907 W. H. Dague Jr., *Navy*
Dexter Draper, *Pennsylvania*
Gus Ziegler, *Pennsylvania*
Adolph Schulz, *Michigan*
William W. Erwin, *Army*
Horatio Biglow, *Yale*
Clarence F. Alcot, *Yale*
T. A. Dwight Jones, *Yale*
John W. Wendell, *Harvard*
Edwin H. W. Harlan, *Princeton*
James M. McCormick, *Princeton*

1908 Hunter Scarlett, *Pennsylvania*
Hamilton Fish, *Harvard*
William A. Goebel, *Yale*
Charles J. Nourse, *Harvard*
Clarke W. Tobin, *Dartmouth*
Mark E. Horr, *Syracuse*
George H. Schildmiller, *Dartmouth*
Walter P. Steffin, *Chicago*
Frederick M. Tibbott, *Princeton*
William A. Hollenbach, *Pennsylvania*
Edward H. Coy, *Yale*

1909 Adrien E. Regnier, *Brown*
Hamilton Fish, *Harvard*
Albert Benbrook, *Michigan*
Carroll T. Cooney, *Yale*
Hamlin F. Andrus, *Yale*
Henry H. Hobbs, *Yale*
John R. Kilpatrick, *Yale*
John McGovern, *Minnesota*
Stephen H. Philben, *Yale*
W. M. Minot, *Harvard*
Edward H. Coy, *Yale*

1910 John R. Kirkpatrick, *Yale*
Robert G. McKay, *Harvard*
Albert Benbrook, *Michigan*
Ernest B. Cozens, *Pennsylvania*
Robert T. Fisher, *Harvard*
James Walker, *Minnesota*
Stanfield Wells, *Michigan*
W. Earl Sprackling, *Brown*
Percy Wendell, *Harvard*
Talbot T. Pendleton, *Princeton*
E. LeRoy Mercer, *Pennsylvania*

1911 Sanford B. White, *Princeton*
Edward J. Hart, *Princeton*
Robert T. Fisher, *Harvard*
Henry H. Ketcham, *Yale*
Joseph M. Duff Jr., *Princeton*
Leland S. Devore, *Army*
Douglass M. Bomeisler, *Yale*
Arthur Howe, *Yale*
Percy Wendell, *Harvard*
Jim Thorpe, *Carlisle*
J. P. Dalton, *Navy*

1912 Samuel M. Felton, *Harvard*
Wesley T. Englehorn, *Dartmouth*
Stanley B. Pennock, *Harvard*
Henry H. Ketcham, *Yale*
W. John Logan, *Princeton*
Robert P. Butler, *Wisconsin*
Douglass M. Bomeisler, *Yale*
George M. Crowther, *Brown*
Charles E. Brickley, *Harvard*
Jim Thorpe, *Carlisle*
E. LeRoy Mercer, *Pennsylvania*

1913 Robert H. Hogsett, *Dartmouth*
Harold R. Ballin, *Princeton*
Stanley B. Pennock, *Harvard*
Paul R. Des Jardien, *Chicago*
J. H. Brown Jr., *Navy*
Nelson S. Talbot, *Yale*
L. A. Merrilat Jr., *Army*
Ellery C. Huntington Jr., *Colgate*
James Claig, *Michigan*
Charles E. Brickley, *Harvard*
Edward W. Mahan, *Harvard*

1914 Huntington Hardwick, *Harvard*
Harold R. Ballin, *Princeton*
Stanley B. Pennock, *Harvard*
John J. McEwan, *Army*
Ralph D. Chapman, *Illinois*
Walter H. Trumbull, *Harvard*
John E. O'Hearn, *Cornell*
Milton P. Ghee, *Dartmouth*
John Maulbetsch, *Michigan*
Frederick J. Bradlee, *Harvard*
Edward W. Mahan, *Harvard*

1915 Bert Baston, *Minnesota*
Joseph A. Gilman, *Harvard*
C. W. Spears, *Dartmouth*
Robert Peck, *Pittsburgh*
Christopher Schlachter, *Syracuse*
Earl C. Abell, *Colgate*
Murray N. Shelton, *Cornell*
Charles Barrett, *Cornell*
Richard S. C. King, *Harvard*
"Bart" Macomber, *Illinois*
Edward W. Mahan, *Harvard*

1916 Bert Baston, *Minnesota*
D. Belford West, *Colgate*
Clinton R. Black Jr., *Yale*
Robert Peck, *Pittsburgh*
Harrie D. Dadmun, *Harvard*
C. E. Homing, *Colgate*
George C. Moseley, *Yale*
O. C. Anderson, *Colgate*
Elmer G. Oliphant, *Army*
Frederick D. Pollard, *Brown*
Charles W. Harley, *Ohio State*

1917 ALL-AMERICA
TEAM
NOT
SELECTED—

WORLD WAR I

1918 Leonard Hilty, *Pittsburgh*
L. A. Alexander, *Syracuse*
Ashel Day, *Georgia Tech*
L. S. Perry, *Navy*
Louis C. Usher, *Syracuse*
Robert Hopper, *Pennsylvania*
Paul Robeson, *Rutgers*
Frank L. Murrey, *Princeton*
Thomas Davies, *Pittsburgh*
Wolcott Roberts, *Navy*
Frank Steketee, *Michigan*

1919 Robert Higgins, *Penn State*
D. Belford West, *Colgate*
L. A. Alexander, *Syracuse*
James R. Weaver, *Centre*
A. F. Youngstrom, *Dartmouth*
Wilbur F. Henry, *Washington & Jefferson*
Henry Miller, *Pennsylvania*
Alvin T. McMillin, *Centre*
Edward Casey, *Harvard*
Charles W. Harley, *Ohio State*
Ira E. Rodgers, *West Virginia*

1920 Charles R. Carney, *Illinois*
J. Stanton Keck, *Princeton*
J. Timothy Callahan, *Yale*
Herbert Stein, *Pittsburgh*
Thomas S. Woods, *Harvard*
Ralph Scott, *Wisconsin*
W. E. Fincher, *Georgia Tech*
Donald B. Lourie, *Princeton*
Gaylord R. Stinchcomb, *Ohio State*
Charles Way, *Penn State*
George Gipp, *Notre Dame*

1921 Harold P. Muller, *California*
Russell F. Stein, *Washington & Jefferson*
Frank J. Schwab, *Lafayette*
Henry Vick, *Michigan*
John F. Brown, *Harvard*
Charles E. McGuire, *Chicago*
James B. Roberts, *Centre*
Aubrey Devine, *Iowa*
Glenn Killinger, *Penn State*
Malcolm P. Aldrich, *Yale*
Edgar L. Kay, *Cornell*

1922 W. H. Taylor, *Navy*
C. Herbert Treat, *Princeton*
Frank J. Schwab, *Lafayette*
Edgar W. Garbisch, *Army*
Charles J. Hubbard, *Harvard*
John Thurman, *Pennsylvania*
Harold P. Muller, *California*
Gordon C. Locke, *Iowa*
Edgar L. Kay, *Cornell*
Harry G. Kipke, *Michigan*
John W. Thomas, *Chicago*

1923 Lynn Bomar, *Vanderbilt*
Century A. Milstead, *Yale*
Charles J. Hubbard, *Harvard*
Jack Balott, *Michigan*
Joseph Bedenk, *Penn State*
Frank L. Sundstrom, *Cornell*
Homer Hazel, *Rutgers*
George R. Pfann, *Cornell*
Harold "Red" Grange, *Illinois*
Earl Martineau, *Minnesota*
William N. Mallory, *Yale*

1924 Henry Bjorkman, *Dartmouth*
Edward McGinley, *Pennsylvania*
Edliff Slaughter, *Michigan*
Edgar Garbisch, *Army*
Edwin Horrell, *California*
Ed Weir, *Nebraska*
Charles Berry, *Lafayette*
Harry Stuhldreher, *Notre Dame*
Harold "Red" Grange, *Illinois*
Walter Koppisch, *Columbia*
Homer Hazel, *Rutgers*

1925 Benjamin Oosterbaan, *Michigan*
Ed Weir, *Nebraska*
Herbert C. Sturhahn, *Yale*
Edward L. McMillan, *Princeton*
Carl H. Diehl, *Dartmouth*
R. E. Chase, *Pittsburgh*
Charles F. Born, *Army*
Harold "Red" Grange, *Illinois*
Andrew J. Oberlander, *Dartmouth*
George Wilson, *Washington*
Ernest Nevers, *Stanford*

1926 Benjamin Oosterbaan, *Michigan*
F. H. Wickhorst, *Navy*
Bernie Shively, *Illinois*
Arthur Boeringer, *Notre Dame*
Herbert C. Sturhahn, *Yale*
Lloyd Yoder, *Carnegie Tech*
Theo E. Shipkey, *Stanford*
Roy E. Randall, *Brown*
Morton Kaer, *Southern California*
Harry E. Wilson, *Army*
Herbert Joesting, *Minnesota*

1927 Benjamin Oosterbaan, *Michigan*
Sidney S. Quarrier, *Yale*
John P. Smith, *Notre Dame*
Lawrence J. Bettencourt, *St. Mary's*
William A. Webster, *Yale*
Jesse Hibbs, *Southern California*
Thomas Nash, *Georgia*
Gilbert Welch, *Pittsburgh*
Christian K. Cagle, *Army*
Morley Drury, *Southern California*
Herbert Joesting, *Minnesota*

1928 Wesley Fesler, *Ohio State*
Albert J. Nowack, *Illinois*
Seraphim Post, *Stanford*
H. R. Pund, *Georgia Tech*
George Gibson, *Minnesota*
Michael Getto, *Pittsburgh*
Irvine Phillips, *California*
Howard Harpster, *Carnegie Tech*
Christian K. Cagle, *Army*
Charles Carroll, *Washington*
Paul Scull, *Pennsylvania*

1929 Francis Tappaan, *Southern California*
Elmer N. Sleight, *Purdue*
John Cannon, *Notre Dame*
Benjamin Ticknor, *Harvard*
Ray Montgomery, *Pittsburgh*
George H. Ackerman, *St. Mary's*
Joseph C. Donchess, *Pittsburgh*
Frank Carideo, *Notre Dame*
Christian K. Cagle, *Army*
Willis B. Banker, *Tulane*
Ralph Welch, *Purdue*

1930 Wesley Fesler, *Ohio State*
Frederick Sington, *Alabama*
Theodore Beckett, *California*
Benjamin Ticknor, *Harvard*
Frederick J. Linehan, *Yale*
Mel Hein, *Washington State*
Gerald Dalrymple, *Tulane*
Frank Carideo, *Notre Dame*
Marty Brill, *Notre Dame*
Reb Russell, *Northwestern*
Erny Pinckert, *Southern California*

1931 John Orsi, *Colgate*
Jesse Quatse, *Pittsburgh*
Clarence Munn, *Minnesota*
Thomas Yarr, *Notre Dame*
John Baker, *Southern California*
John Riley, *Northwestern*
Gerald Dalrymple, *Tulane*
Gaius Shaver, *Southern California*
Marchmont Schwartz, *Notre Dame*
Ernest Rentner, *Northwestern*
John Lewis Cain, *Alabama*

1932 Paul Moss, *Purdue*
Joseph Kurth, *Notre Dame*
Robert Smith, *Colgate*
Arthur Krueger, *Marquette*
William Corbus, *Stanford*
Ernest Smith, *Southern California*
Fred Petoskey, *Michigan*
Harry Newman, *Michigan*
James Hitchcock, *Auburn*
Warren Heller, *Pittsburgh*
Roy Horstmann, *Purdue*

1933 Joseph P. Skladany, *Pittsburgh*
Francis Wistert, *Michiigan*
Aaron Rosenberg, *Southern California*
Charles Bernard, *Michigan*
William Corbus, *Stanford*
C. B. Ceppi, *Princeton*
William Smith, *Washington*
Irving Warburton, *Southern California*
Duane Purvis, *Purdue*
Beattie Feathers, *Tennessee*
George H. Sauer, *Nebraska*

1934 Donald Hutson, *Alabama*
George W. Maddox, *Kansas State*
George Barclay, *North Carolina*
John Robinson, *Notre Dame*
C. C. Hartwig, *Pittsburgh*
Regis Monohan, *Notre Dame*
Millard Howell, *Alabama*
James Moscrip, *Stanford*
Francis Lund, *Minnesota*
Jay Berwanger, *Chicago*
Robert Grayson, *Stanford*

1935 Wayne Millner, *Notre Dame*
Lawrence Lutz, *California*
J. C. Wetsel, *Southern Methodist*
Gomer Jones, *Ohio State*
Darrell G. Lester, *Texas Christian*
Edwin Widseth, *Minnesota*
James Moscrip, *Stanford*
Riley Smith, *Alabama*
Jay Berwanger, *Chicago*
William Shakespeare, *Notre Dame*
Robert Grayson, *Stanford*

1936 Gaynell Tinsley, *Louisiana State*
Edwin Widseth, *Minnesota*
Max Starcevich, *Washington*
Michael J. Basrak, *Duquesne*
Stephen Reid, *Northwestern*
Frank Kinard, *Mississippi*
Lawrence Kelley, *Yale*
Nello Falaschi, *Santa Clara*
Clarence Parker, *Duke*
Kent Ryan, *Utah State*
Samuel Francis, *Nebraska*

1937 Perry Schwartz, *California*
Edward Beinor, *Notre Dame*
Leroy Monsky, *Alabama*
Alex Wojciechowicz, *Fordham*
Gust Zarnas, *Ohio State*
Anthony F. Matisi, *Pittsburgh*
Raymond King, *Minnesota*
Clinton Frank, *Yale*
Marshall Goldberg, *Pittsburgh*
Samuel Chapman, *California*
Corby Davis, *Indiana*

1938 Earl M. Brown, *Notre Dame*
Edward Beinor, *Notre Dame*
Harry Smith, *Southern California*
Daniel Hill, *Duke*
Ralph Heikkinen, *Michigan*
Robert Voigts, *Northwestern*
Bowden Wyatt, *Tennessee*
Victor Bottari, *California*
David O'Brien, *Texas Christian*
Robert MacLead, *Dartmouth*
Marshall Goldberg, *Pittsburgh*

1939 William Kerr, *Notre Dame*
Nicholas Drahos, *Cornell*
Harry Smith, *Southern California*
John Schiechl, *Santa Clara*
Esco Sarkinen, *Ohio State*
James W. Reeder, *Illinois*
Edward Molinski, *Tennessee*
Paul Christman, *Missouri*
Nile Kinnick, *Iowa*
Thomas Harmon, *Michigan*
John Kimbrough, *Texas A & M*

1940 Eugene Goodreault, *Boston College*
Nicholas Drahos, *Cornell*
Robert Suffridge, *Tennessee*
Rudolph Mucha, *Washington*
David W. Rankin, *Purdue*
Alfred Bauman, *Northwestern*
Marshall Robnett, *Texas A & M*
Frank C. Albert, *Stanford*
George H. Franck, *Minnesota*
Thomas Harmon, *Michigan*
John Kimbrough, *Texas A & M*

1941 Robert Dove, *Notre Dame*
Alfred Bauman, *Northwestern*
Endicott Peabody, *Harvard*
Darrell Jenkins, *Missouri*
Raymond Frankowski, *Washington*
Richard Wildung, *Minnesota*
Holt Rast, *Alabama*
Frank C. Albert, *Stanford*
Bruce Smith, *Minnesota*
Frank Sinkwich, *Georgia*
Robert Westfall, *Michigan*

1942 David Schreiner, *Wisconsin*
Richard Wildung, *Minnesota*
Lindell L. Houston, *Ohio State*
Joseph Damnanoich, *Alabama*
Charles Taylor, *Stanford*
Al Wistert, *Michigan*
Robert Dove, *Notre Dame*
Paul Governali, *Columbia*
Frank Sinkwich, *Georgia*
William Hillenbrand, *Indiana*
Marlin Harder, *Wisconsin*

1943 Ralph Heywood, *Southern California*
Peter Pihos, *Indiana*
James J. White, *Notre Dame*
Casimir Myslinski, *Army*
John W. Weber, *Georgia Tech*
Donald B. Whitmire, *Navy*
John Yonakor, *Notre Dame*
Creighton Miller, *Notre Dame*
Angelo Bertelli, *Notre Dame*
Otto Graham, *Northwestern*
William Daley, *Michigan*

1944 Philip Tinsley, *Georgia Tech*
Donald B. Whitmire, *Navy*
William C. Hackett, *Ohio State*
Caleb Warrington, *Auburn*
Benjamin S. Chase, *Navy*
John Ferraro, *Southern California*
John Dugger, *Ohio State*
Leslie Horvath, *Ohio State*
Robert T. Jenkins, *Navy*
Glenn W. Davis, *Army*
Felix A. Blanchard, *Army*

1945 Max Morris, *Northwestern*
DeWitt Coulter, *Army*
John F. Green, *Army*
Richard Scott, *Navy*
Warren E. Amling, *Ohio State*
George Savitsky, *Pennsylvania*
H. Richard Duden Jr., *Navy*
Herman Wedemeyer, *St. Mary's*
Robert Fenimore, *Oklahoma A. & M.*
Glenn W. Davis, *Army*
Felix A. Blanchard, *Army*

1946 Burr Baldwin, *UCLA*
George Connor, *Notre Dame*
Alex Agase, *Illinois*
Paul Duke, *Georgia Tech*
Weldon Humble, *Rice*
Richard Huffman, *Tennessee*
Hubert Bechtol, *Texas*
John Lujack, *Notre Dame*
Charles Trippi, *Georgia*
Glenn Davis, *Army*
Felix Blanchard, *Army*

1947 George B. Poole, *Mississippi*
George Connor, *Notre Dame*
Joseph Steffy, *Army*
Charles Bednarik, *Pennsylvania*
William Swiacki, *Columbia*
John Ferraro, *Southern California*
Rodney Franz, *California*
John Lujack, *Notre Dame*
Robert Chappuis, *Michigan*
Doak Walker, *Southern Methodist*
Anthony Minisi, *Pennsylvania*

1948 Richard Rifenburg, *Michigan*
Alvin L. Wistert, *Michigan*
William Fischer, *Notre Dame*
Charles Bednarik, *Pennsylvania*
Paul Burris, *Oklahoma*
Leo Nomellini, *Minnesota*
Leon Hart, *Notre Dame*
John Rauch, *Georgia*
Doak Walker, *Southern Methodist*
Charles Justice, *North Carolina*
Jack Jensen, *California*

1949 Froggy Williams, *Rice* (E)
Leon Hart, *Notre Dame* (E)
Leo Nomellini, *Minnesota* (T)
Alvin Wistert, *Michigan* (T)
Rod Franz, *California* (G)
Ed Bagdon, *Michigan State* (G)
Clayton Tonnemaker, *Minnesota* (C)
Doak Walker, *Southern Methodist* (B)
Arnold Galiffa, *Army* (B)
Bob Williams, *Notre Dame* (B)
Emil Sitko, *Notre Dame* (B)

1950 Bill McColl, *Stanford* (E)
Dan Foldberg, *Army* (E)
Bob Gain, *Kentucky* (T)
Jim Weatherall, *Oklahoma* (T)
Les Richter, *California* (G)
Lewis McFadin, *Texas* (G)
Jerry Groom, *Notre Dame* (C)
Vito Parilli, *Kentucky* (B)
Vic Janowicz, *Ohio State* (B)
Kyle Rote, *Southern Methodist* (B)
Leon Heath, *Oklahoma* (B)

1951 Bill McColl, *Stanford* (E)
Robert Carey, *Michigan State* (E)
Don Coleman, *Michigan State* (T)
Jim Weatherall, *Oklahoma,* (T)
Robert Ward, *Maryland* (G)
Les Richter, *California* (G)
Dick Hightower, *Southern Methodist* (C)
Vito Parilli, *Kentucky* (B)
Henry Lauricella, *Tennessee* (B)
Richard Kazmaier, *Princeton* (B)
John Karras, *Illinois* (B)

1952 Frank McPhee, *Princeton* (E)
Bernard Flowers, *Purdue* (E)
Richard Modzelewski, *Maryland* (T)
Harold Miller, *Georgia Tech* (T)
Elmer Willhoite, *Southern California* (G)
John Michels, *Tennessee* (G)
Donn Moomaw, *UCLA* (C)
John Scarbath, *Maryland* (B)
John Lattner, *Notre Dame* (B)
Jim Sears, *Southern California* (B)
William Vessels, *Oklahoma* (B)

1953 Don Dohoney, *Michigan State* (E)
Carlton Massey, *Texas* (E)
Stanley Jones, *Maryland* (T)
Arthur Hunter, *Notre Dame* (T)
J. D. Roberts, *Oklahoma* (G)
Crawford Mims, *Mississippi* (G)
Lawrence Morris, *Georgia Tech* (C)
John Lattner, *Notre Dame* (B)
Paul Giel, *Minnesota* (B)
Paul Cameron, *UCLA* (B)
James C. Caroline, *Illinois* (B)

1954 Max Boydston, *Oklahoma* (E)
Ron Beagle, *Navy* (E)
Jack Ellena, *UCLA* (T)
Sidney Fournet, *Louisiana State* (T)
Bud Brooks, *Arkansas* (G)
Calvin Jones, *Iowa* (G)
Kurt Burris, *Oklahoma* (C)
Ralph Guglielmi, *Notre Dame* (B)
Richard Moegle, *Rice* (B)
Howard Cassady, *Ohio State* (B)
Alan Ameche, *Wisconsin* (B)

1955 Ron Beagle, *Navy* (E)
Ron Kramer, *Michigan* (E)
Bruce Bosley, *West Virginia* (T)
Norman Masters, *Michigan State* (T)
Bo Bolinger, *Oklahoma* (G)
Calvin Jones, *Iowa* (G)
Robert Pellegrini, *Maryland* (C)
Howard Cassady, *Ohio State* (B)
James Swink, *Texas Christian* (B)
Earl Morrall, *Michigan State* (B)
Paul Hornung, *Notre Dame* (B)

1956 Joseph Walton, *Pittsburgh* (E)
Ron Kramer, *Michigan* (E)
John Witte, *Oregon State* (T)
Lou Michaels, *Kentucky* (T)
James Parker, *Ohio State* (G)
William Glass, *Baylor* (G)
Jerry Tubbs, *Oklahoma* (C)
James Brown, *Syracuse* (B)
Johnny Majors, *Tennessee* (B)
Thomas McDonald, *Oklahoma* (B)
John Brodie, *Stanford* (B)

1957 Jim Phillips, *Auburn* (E)
Dick Wallen, *UCLA* (E)
Lou Michaels, *Kentucky* (T)
Alex Karras, *Iowa* (T)
William Krisher, *Oklahoma* (G)
Al Ecuyer, *Notre Dame* (G)
Daniel Currie, *Michigan State* (C)
John David Crow, *Texas A & M* (B)
Walter Kowalczyk, *Michigan State* (B)
Robert Anderson, *Army* (B)
Clendon Thomas, *Oklahoma* (B)

1958 Gilbert Dial, *Rice* (E)
Samuel Williams, *Michigan State* (E)
Theodore Bates, *Oregon State* (T)
Brock Strom, *Air Force* (T)
John Guzik, *Pittsburgh* (G)
Zeke Smith, *Auburn* (G)
Robert Harrison, *Oklahoma* (C)
Randolph Duncan, *Iowa* (B)
Peter Dawkins, *Army* (B)
William Cannon, *Louisiana State* (B)
Robert White, *Ohio State* (B)

1959 William Carpenter, *Army* (E)
Montford Stickles, *Notre Dame* (E)
Donald Floyd, *Texas Christian* (T)
Daniel Lanphear, *Wisconsin* (T)
Roger Davis, *Syracuse* (G)
William Burrell, *Illinois* (G)
Maxie Baughan, *Georgia Tech* (C)
Richard Lucas, *Penn State* (B)
William Cannon, *Louisiana State* (B)
Ronald Burton, *Northwestern* (B)
Charles Flowers, *Mississippi* (B)

1960 Michael Ditka, *Pittsburgh* (E)
Daniel LaRose, *Missouri* (E)
Robert Lilly, *Texas Christian* (T)
Kenneth Rice, *Auburn* (T)
Joseph Romig, *Colorado* (G)
Tom Brown, *Minnesota* (G)
Emil Holub, *Texas Tech* (C)
Jake Gibbs, *Mississippi* (B)
Joseph Bellino, *Navy* (B)
Ernest Davis, *Syracuse* (B)
Robert Ferguson, *Ohio State* (B)

1961 Gary Collins, *Maryland* (E)
William Miller, *Miami* (E)
William Neighbors, *Alabama* (T)
Merlin Olsen, *Utah State* (T)
Roy Winston, *Louisiana State* (G)
Joseph Romig, *Colorado* (G)
Alexander Kroll, *Rutgers* (C)
Ernest Davis, *Syracuse* (B)
Robert Ferguson, *Ohio State* (B)
James Saxton, *Texas* (B)
Sandy Stephens, *Minnesota* (B)

1962 Harold Bedsole, Southern California (E)
Pat Richter, *Wisconsin* (E)
Robert Bell, *Minnesota* (T)
James Dunaway, *Mississippi* (T)
Jack Cvercko, *Northwestern* (G)
John Treadwell, *Texas* (G)
Lee Roy Jordan, *Alabama* (C)
Terry Baker, *Oregon State* (B)
Melvin Renfro, *Oregon* (B)
George Saimes, *Michigan State* (B)
Jerry Stovall, *Louisiana State* (B)

1963 Vern Burke, *Oregon State* (E)
Lawrence Elkins, *Baylor* (E)
Scott Appleton, *Texas* (T)
Carl Eller, *Minnesota* (T)
Robert Brown, *Nebraska* (G)
Rick Redman, *Washington* (G)
Richard Butkus, *Illinois* (C)
Roger Staubach, *Navy* (B)
Sherman Lewis, *Michigan State* (B)
Gale Sayers, *Kansas* (B)
Paul Martha, *Pittsburgh* (B)

1964 Jack Snow, *Notre Dame* (E)
Frederick Biletnikoff, *Florida State* (E)
Larry Kramer, *Minnesota* (T)
Ralph Neely, *Oklahoma* (T)
Rick Redman, *Washington* (G)
Glenn Ressler, *Penn State* (G)
Richard Butkus, *Illinois* (C)
John Huarte, *Notre Dame* (B)
Gale Sayers, *Kansas* (B)
Lawrence Elkins, *Baylor* (B)
Tucker Frederickson, *Auburn* (B)

1965 **OFFENSIVE TEAM**
Harold Twilley, *Tulsa* (E)
Freeman White, *Nebraska* (E)
Sam Ball, *Kentucky* (T)
Glen Hines, *Arkansas* (T)
Richard Arrington, *Notre Dame* (G)
Stas Maliszewski, *Princeton* (G)
Paul Crane, *Alabama* (C)
Robert Griese, *Purdue* (B)
Donny Anderson, *Texas Tech* (B)
Michael Garrett, *Southern California* (B)
James Grabowski, *Illinois* (B)

DEFENSIVE TEAM
Aaron Brown, *Minnesota* (E)
Charles Smith, *Michigan State* (E)
Walter Barnes, *Nebraska* (T)
Loyd Phillips, *Arkansas* (T)
Carl McAdams, *Oklahoma* (MG)
William Yearby, *Michigan* (LB)
Thomas Nobis, *Texas* (LB)
Frank Emanuel, *Tennessee* (LB)
George Webster, *Michigan State* (B)
Johnny Roland, *Missouri* (B)
Nicholas Rassas, *Notre Dame* (B)

1966 **OFFENSIVE TEAM**
Jack Clancy, *Michigan* (E)
Raymond Perkins, *Alabama* (E)
Cecil Dowdy, *Alabama* (T)
Ron Yary, *Southern California* (T)
Thomas Regner, *Notre Dame* (G)
LaVerne Allers, *Nebraska* (G)
James Breland, *Georgia Tech* (C)
Steven Spurrier, *Florida* (B)
Floyd Little, *Syracuse* (B)
Clinton Jones, *Michigan State* (B)
Nicholas Eddy, *Notre Dame* (B)

DEFENSIVE TEAM
Alan Page, *Notre Dame* (E)
Charles Smith, *Michigan State* (E)
Loyd Phillips, *Arkansas* (T)
Thomas Greenlee, *Washington* (T)
John LaGrone, *Southern Methodist* (MG)
Wayne Meylan, *Nebraska* (LB)
Paul Naumoff, *Tennessee* (LB)
James Lynch, *Notre Dame* (LB)
George Webster, *Michigan State* (B)
Thomas Beier, *Miami* (Fla.) (B)
Nate Shaw, *Southern California* (B)

1967 **OFFENSIVE TEAM**
Dennis Homan, *Alabama* (E)
Jim Seymour, *Notre Dame* (E)
Edgar Chandler, *Georgia* (T)
Ron Yary, *USC* (T)
Gary Cassells, *Indiana* (G)
Harry Olzewski, *Clemson* (G)
Bob Johnson, *Tennessee* (C)
Gary Beban, *UCLA* (QB)
Larry Csonka, *Syracuse* (B)
Leroy Keyes, *Purdue* (B)
O. J. Simpson, *USC* (B)

DEFENSIVE TEAM
Ted Hendricks, *Miami* (E)
Bob Stein, *Minnesota* (E)
Dennis Byrd, *North Carolina State* (T)
Kevin Hardy, *Notre Dame* (T)
Granville Liggins, *Oklahoma* (MG)
Don Manning, *UCLA* (LB)
Wayne Meylan, *Nebraska* (LB)
Adrian Young, *USC* (LB)
Bobby Johns, *Alabama* (B)
Tom Schoen, *Notre Dame* (B)
Frank Loria, *VPI* (S)

1968 **OFFENSIVE TEAM**
Jim Seymour, *Notre Dame* (E)
Ted Kwalick, *Penn State* (E)
Dave Foley, *Ohio State* (T)
George Kunz, *Notre Dame* (T)
Guy Dennis, *Florida* (G)
Charles Rosenfelder, *Tennessee* (G)
John Didion, *Oregon State* (C)
Jerry Levias, *SMU* (FL)
Terry Hanratty, *Notre Dame* (QB)
Leroy Keyes, *Purdue* (B)
O. J. Simpson, *USC* (B)

DEFENSIVE TEAM
Ted Hendricks, *Miami* (E)
Bob Stein, *Minnesota* (E)
Bill Stanfill, *Georgia* (T)
Joe Greene, *North Texas State* (T)
Chuck Kyle, *Purdue* (MG)
Dennis Onkotz, *Penn State* (LB)
Mike Hall, *Alabama* (LB)
Jake Scott, *Georgia* (B)
Roger Wehrli, *Missouri* (B)
Tony Kyasky, *Syracuse* (B)
Mike Battle, *USC* (S)

1969 OFFENSIVE TEAM

Jim Mandich, *Michigan* (E)
Charles Speyrer, *Texas* (E)
Sid Smith, *USC* (T)
Bob McKay, *Texas* (T)
Larry DiNardo, *Notre Dame* (G)
Chip Kell, *Tennessee* (G)
Rodney Brand, *Arkansas* (C)
Mike Phipps, *Purdue* (QB)
Carlos Alvarez, *Florida* (FL)
Steve Owens, *Oklahoma* (B)
Jim Otis, *Ohio State* (B)

DEFENSIVE TEAM

Jim Gunn, *USC* (E)
Phil Olsen, *Utah State* (E)
Mike Reid, *Penn State* (T)
Mike McCoy, *Notre Dame* (T)
Jim Stillwagon, *Ohio State* (MG)
Dennis Onkotz, *Penn State* (LB)
Steve Kiner, *Tennessee* (LB)
Mike Ballou, *UCLA* (LB)
Jack Tatum, *Ohio State* (B)
Tom Curtis, *Michigan* (B)
Buddy McClinton, *Auburn* (B)

1970 OFFENSIVE TEAM

Chuck Dicus, *Arkansas* (E)
Tom Gatewood, *Notre Dame* (E)
Cotton Speyrer, *Texas* (E)
Dan Dierdorf, *Michigan* (T)
Bobby Weunsch, *Texas* (T)
Larry DiNardo, *Notre Dame* (G)
Chip Kell, *Tennessee* (G)
Don Popplewell, *Colorado* (C)
Jim Plunkett, *Stamford* (QB)
John Musso, *Alabama* (B)
Don McCauley, *North Carolina* (B)
Steve Worster, *Texas* (B)

DEFENSIVE TEAM

Jack Youngblood, *Florida* (E)
Charles Weaver, *USC* (E)
Rock Perdoni, *Georgia Tech* (T)
Tom Neville, *Yale* (T)
Jim Stillwagon, *Ohio State* (MG)
Jerry Murtaugh, *Nebraska* (LB)
Jack Ham, *Penn State* (LB)
Larry Willingham, *Auburn* (B)
Pat Murphy, *Colorado* (B)
Murray Bowden, *Dartmouth* (B)
Jack Tatum, *Ohio State* (B)

1971 OFFENSIVE TEAM

Terry Beasley, *Auburn* (E)
Johnny Rodgers, *Nebraska* (E)
Jerry Sisemore, *Texas* (T)
Dave Joyner, *Penn State* (T)
Reggie McKenzie, *Michigan* (G)
Royce Smith, *Georgia* (G)
Tom Brahaney, *Oklahoma* (C)
Pat Sullivan, *Auburn* (QB)
Johnny Musso, *Alabama* (B)
Ed Marinaro, *Cornell* (B)
Greg Pruitt, *Oklahoma* (B)

DEFENSIVE TEAM

Walt Patulski, *Notre Dame* (E)
Willie Harper, *Nebraska* (E)
Sherman White, *California* (T)
Herb Orvis, *Colorado* (T)
Rich Glover, *Nebraska* (MG)
Mike Taylor, *Michigan* (LB)
Jackie Walker, *Tennessee* (LB)
Tommy Casanova, *LSU* (B)
Bobby Majors, *Tennessee* (B)
Clarance Ellis, *Notre Dame* (B)
Dickie Harris, *South Carolina* (B)

1972 OFFENSIVE TEAM

Charles Young, *USC* (TE)
Jerry Sisemore, *Texas* (T)
John Hicks, *Ohio State* (T)
John Hannah, *Alabama* (G)
Skip Singletary, *Temple* (G)
Tom Brahaney, *Oklahoma* (C)
John Hufnagel, *Penn State* (QB)
Greg Pruitt, *Oklahoma* (B)
Dick Jauron, *Yale* (B)
Otis Armstrong, *Purdue* (B)
Johnny Rodgers, *Nebraska* (WR)

DEFENSIVE TEAM

Willie Harper, *Nebraska* (E)
Bruce Bannon, *Penn State* (E)
Dave Butz, *Purdue* (T)
Greg Marx, *Notre Dame* (T)
Rich Glover, *Nebraska* (MG)
Steve Brown, *Oregon State* (LB)
Tom Jackson, *Louisville* (LB)
Ray Guy, *Southern Mississippi* (B)
Bob Popelka, *Southern Methodist* (B)
Brad Van Pelt, *Michigan State* (B)
Randy Logan, *Michigan* (B)

1973 OFFENSIVE TEAM

Dave Casper, *Notre Dame* (TE)
Wayne Wheeler, *Alabama* (WR)
John Hicks, *Ohio State* (T)
Eddie Foster, *Oklahoma* (T)
Tyler Lafauci, *Louisiana State* (G)
Bill Yoest, *North Carolina State* (G)
Bill Wyman, *Texas* (C)
David Jaynes, *Kansas* (QB)
John Cappeletti, *Penn State* (RB)
Roosevelt Leaks, *Texas* (RB)
Woody Green, *Arizona State* (RB)

DEFENSIVE TEAM

Lucius Selmon, *Oklahoma* (L)
Dave Gallagher, *Michigan* (L)
John Dutton, *Nebraska* (L)
Charlie Hall, *Tulane* (L)
Tony Christiani, *Miami* (MG)
Randy Gradishar, *Ohio State* (LB)
Richard Wood, *USC* (LB)
Ed O'Neil, *Penn State* (LB)
Mike Townsend, *Notre Dame* (B)
Artimus Parker, *USC* (B)
Randy Rhino, *Georgia Tech* (B)

1974 OFFENSIVE TEAM

Patrick McInally, *Harvard* (WR)
Peter Demmerle, *Notre Dame* (WR)
Kurt Schumacher, *Ohio State* (T)
Robert Simmons, *Texas* (T)
John Nessel, *Penn State* (G)
Kenneth Huff, *North Carolina* (G)
Geoff Reece, *Washington State* (C)
Steve Joachim, *Temple* (QB)
Joseph Washington, *Oklahoma* (RB)
Archie Griffin, *Ohio State* (RB)
Anthony Davis, *USC* (RB)

DEFENSIVE TEAM

Mack Mitchell, *Houston* (E)
James Webb, *Mississippi State* (E)
Randy White, *Maryland* (T)
Michael Fanning, *Notre Dame* (T)
Gary Burley, *Pittsburgh* (MG)
Rod Shoate, *Oklahoma* (LB)
Woodrow Lowe, *Alabama* (LB)
Kenneth Bernich, *Auburn* (LB)
John Provost, *Holy Cross* (B)
Dave Brown, *Michigan* (B)
Randy Rhino, *Georgia Tech* (B)

1975 OFFENSIVE TEAM

Bennie Cunningham, *Clemson* (TE)
Steve Rivera, *California* (WR)
Dennis Lick, *Wisconsin* (T)
Bob Simmons, *Texas* (T)
Terry Webb, *Oklahoma* (G)
Randy Johnson, *Georgia* (G)
Rik Bonness, *Nebraska* (C)
John Sciarra, *UCLA* (QB)
Archie Griffin, *Ohio State* (RB)
Ricky Bell, *USC* (RB)
Tony Dorsett, *Pittsburgh* (RB)
Chunk Muncie, *California* (RB)

DEFENSIVE TEAM

Leroy Cook, *Alabama* (E)
Jimbo Elrod, *Oklahoma* (E)
Leroy Selmon, *Oklahoma* (T)
Steve Niehaus, *Notre Dame* (T)
Dewey Selmon, *Oklahoma* (MG)
Ed Simonini, *Texas A & M* (LB)
Greg Buttle, *Penn State* (LB)
Don Dufek, *Michigan* (LB)
Chet Moeller, *Navy* (B)
Pat Thomas, *Texas A & M* (B)
Tim Fox, *Ohio State* (B)
Chris Bahr, *Penn State* (K)

1976 OFFENSIVE TEAM

Larry Seiver, *Tennessee* (SE)
Ken MacAfee, *Notre Dame* (TE)
Warren Bryant, *Kentucky* (T)
Mike Vaughan, *Oklahoma* (T)
Mark Donahue, *Michigan* (G)
Joel Parrish, *Georgia* (G)
Bill Bryan, *Duke* (C)
Tommy Kramer, *Rice* (QB)
Tony Dorsett, *Pittsburgh* (RB)
Ricky Bell, *USC* (RB)
Rob Lytle, *Michigan* (RB)

DEFENSIVE TEAM

Ross Browner, *Notre Dame* (E)
Duncan McColl, *Stanford* (E)
Wilson Whitely, *Houston* (T)
Mike Fultz, *Nebraska* (T)
Al Romano, *Pittsburgh* (MG)
Calvin O'Neal, *Michigan* (LB)
Robert Jackson, *Texas A & M* (LB)
Thomas Howard, *Texas Tech* (LB)
Luther Bradley, *Notre Dame* (B)
Bill Armstrong, *Wake Forest* (B)
Dennis Thurman, *USC* (B)
Dave Butterfield, *Nebraska* (B)

1977 OFFENSIVE TEAM

Ossie Newsome, *Alabama* (SE)
Ken MacAfee, *Notre Dame* (TE)
Chris Ward, *Ohio State* (T)
Dan Irons, *Texas Tech* (T)
Mark Donahue, *Michigan* (G)
Leotis Harris, *Arkansas* (G)
Doug Williams, *Grambling State* (QB)
Tom Brzoza, *Pittsburgh* (C)
Earl Campbell, *Texas* (B)
Terry Miller, *Oklahoma State* (B)
Charles Alexander, *LSU* (B)
John Pagliaro, *Yale* (B)

DEFENSIVE TEAM

Ross Browner, *Notre Dame* (E)
Art Still, *Kentucky* (E)
Brad Shearer, *Texas* (T)
Randy Holloway, *Pittsburgh* (T)
Aaron Brown, *Ohio State* (MG)
Jerry Robinson, *UCLA* (LB)
Tom Cousineau, *Ohio State* (LB)
Darryl Hunt, *Oklahoma* (LB)
Luther Bradley, *Notre Dame* (B)
Zack Henderson, *Oklahoma* (B)
Dennis Thurman, *USC* (B)
Bob Jury, *Pittsburgh* (B)

1978 OFFENSIVE TEAM

Emanuel Tolbert, *SMU* (WR)
Kellen Winslow, *Missouri* (TE)
Kelvin Clark, *Nebraska* (T)
Keith Dorney, *Penn State* (T)
Pat Howell, *USC* (G)
Greg Roberts, *Oklahoma* (G)
Dave Huffman, *Notre Dame* (C)
Chuck Fusina, *Penn State* (QB)
Billy Sims, *Oklahoma* (RB)
Charles White, *USC* (RB)
Charles Alexander, *LSU* (RB)
Matt Bahr, *Penn State* (PK)

DEFENSIVE TEAM

Al Harris, *Arizona State* (E)
Hugh Green, *Pittsburgh* (E)
Matt Millen, *Penn State* (T)
Mike Bell, *Colorado State* (T)
Reggie Kinlaw, *Oklahoma* (MG)
Jerry Robinson, *UCLA* (LB)
Tom Cousineau, *Ohio State* (LB)
Bob Golic, *Notre Dame* (LB)
Jeff Nixon, *Richmond* (B)
Ken Easley, *UCLA* (B)
Johnnie Johnson, *Texas* (B)
Russell Erxleben, *Texas* (K)

1979 OFFENSIVE TEAM

Ken Margerum, *Stanford* (WR)
Junior Miller, *Nebraska* (TE)
Greg Kolenda, *Arkansas* (T)
Melvin Jones, *Houston* (T)
Brad Budde, *USC* (G)
Ken Fritz, *Ohio State* (G)
Jim Ritcher, *North Carolina State* (C)
Marc Wilson, *Brigham Young* (QB)
Charles White, *USC* (B)
Billy Sims, *Oklahoma* (B)
Vagas Ferguson, *Notre Dame* (B)
Dale Castro, *Maryland* (PK)

DEFENSIVE TEAM

Hugh Green, *Pittsburgh* (E)
Jacob Green, *Texas A & M* (E)
Steve McMichael, *Texas* (T)
Bruce Clark, *Penn State* (T)
Ron Simmons, *Florida State* (MG)
George Cumby, *Oklahoma* (LB)
Mike Singletary, *Baylor* (LB)
Ron Simpkins, *Michigan* (LB)
Ken Easley, *UCLA* (B)
Roland James, *Tennessee* (B)
Johnnie Johnson, *Texas* (B)
Jim Miller, *Mississippi* (P)

1980 OFFENSIVE TEAM

Ken Margerum, *Stanford* (WR)
Dave Young, *Purdue* (TE)
Louis Oubre, *Oklahoma* (T)
Mark May, *Pittsburgh* (T)
Randy Schleusener, *Nebraska* (G)
Ron Wooten, *North Carolina* (G)
George Lilja, *Michigan* (C)
Mark Herrmann, *Purdue* (QB)
George Rogers, *South Carolina* (B)
Herschel Walker, *Georgia* (B)
Jarvis Redwine, *Nebraska* (B)
Rex Robinson, *Georgia* (PK)

DEFENSIVE TEAM

Hugh Green, *Pittsburgh* (E)
E. J. Junior, *Alabama* (E)
Len Mitchell, *Houston* (T)
Hosca Taylor, *Houston* (T)
Ron Simmons, *Florida State* (MG)
Mike Singletary, *Baylor* (LB)
Tom Boyd, *Alabama* (LB)
Bob Crable, *Notre Dame* (LB)
Ken Easley, *UCLA* (B)
Ron Lott, *USC* (B)
Scott Woerner, *Georgia* (B)
Ray Stachowicz, *Michigan State* (P)

1981 **OFFENSIVE TEAM**
Anthony Carter, *Michigan* (WR)
Tim Wrightman, *UCLA* (TE)
Terry Tausch, *Texas* (T)
William "Bubba" Paris, *Michigan* (T)
Sean Farrell, *Penn State* (G)
Roy Foster, *USC* (G)
Dave Rimington, *Nebraska* (C)
Dan Marino, *Pittsburgh* (QB)
Marcus Allen, *USC* (B)
Herschel Walker, *Georgia* (B)
Curt Warner, *Penn State* (B)
Morten Anderson, *Michigan State* (PK)

DEFENSIVE TEAM
Billy Ray Smith, *Arkansas* (E)
Jimmy Williams, *Nebraska* (E)
Kenneth Sims, *Texas* (T)
Lester Williams, *Miami* (Fla.) (T)
Tim Krumrie, *Wisconsin* (MG)
Bob Crable, *Notre Dame* (LB)
Tom Boyd, *Alabama* (LB)
Chip Banks, *USC* (LB)
Vann McElroy, *Baylor* (B)
Mike Richardson, *Arizona State* (B)
Tommy Wilcox, *Alabama* (B)
Reggie Roby, *Iowa* (P)

1982 **OFFENSIVE TEAM**
Anthony Carter, *Michigan* (WR)
Gordon Hudson, *Brigham Young* (TE)
Don Mosebar, *USC* (T)
Jimbo Covert, *Pittsburgh* (T)
Bruce Matthews, *USC* (G)
Dave Drechshler, *North Carolina* (G)
Dave Rimington, *Nebraska* (C)
John Elway, *Stanford* (QB)
Herschel Walker, *Georgia* (B)
Eric Dickerson, *SMU* (B)
Ernest Anderson, *Oklahoma State* (B)
Chuck Nelson, *Washington* (PK)

DEFENSIVE TEAM
Billy Ray Smith, *Arkansas* (DL)
Jimmy Payne, *Georgia* (DL)
Tim Krumrie, *Wisconsin* (DL)
George Achica, *USC* (DL)
Mark Stewart, *Washington* (LB)
Marcus Marek, *Ohio State* (LB)
Vernon Maxwell, *Arizona State* (LB)
Mike Richardson, *Arizona State* (B)
Terry Hoage, *Georgia* (B)
Tommy Wilcox, *Alabama* (B)
Terry Kinard, *Clemson* (B)
Reggie Roby, *Iowa* (P)

1983 **OFFENSIVE TEAM**
Irving Fryar, *Nebraska* (WR)
Gordon Hudson, *Brigham Young* (TE)
Bill Fralic, *Pittsburgh* (T)
Terry Long, *East Carolina* (T)
Dean Steinkuhler, *Nebraska* (G)
Doug Dawson, *Texas* (G)
Tony Slaton, *USC* (C)
Steve Young, *Brigham Young* (QB)
Mike Rozier, *Nebraska* (B)
Greg Allen, *Florida State* (B)
Napoleon McCallum, *Navy* (B)
Luis Zendejas, *Arizona State* (PK)

DEFENSIVE TEAM
Rick Bryan, *Oklahoma* (DL)
William Fuller, *North Carolina* (DL)
Reggie White, *Tennessee* (DL)
William Perry, *Clemson* (DL)
Jeff Leiding, *Texas* (LB)
Ricky Hunley, *Arizona* (LB)
Wilbur Marshall, *Florida* (LB)
Don Rogers, *UCLA* (B)
Mossy Cade, *Texas* (B)
Russell Carter, *SMU* (B)
Terry Hoage, *Georgia* (B)
Jim Colquitt, *Tennessee* (P)

1984 **OFFENSIVE TEAM**
David Williams, *Illinois* (WR)
Bob Bennett, *West Virginia* (TE)
Bill Fralic, *Pittsburgh* (T)
Lomas Brown, *Florida* (T)
Bill Mayo, *Tennessee* (G)
Del Wilkes, *South Carolina* (G)
Mark Traynowicz, *Nebraska* (C)
Doug Flutie, *Boston College* (QB)
Keith Byars, *Ohio State* (B)
Greg Allen, *Florida State* (B)
Ken Davis, *TCU* (B)
Kevin Butler, *Georgia* (PK)

DEFENSIVE TEAM
William Perry, *Clemson* (DL)
Tony Degrave, *Texas* (DL)
Bruce Smith, *Virginia Tech* (DL)
Ron Holmes, *Washington* (DL)
Jack Del Rio, *USC* (LB)
Larry Station, *Iowa* (LB)
Gregg Carr, *Auburn* (LB)
Jeff Sanchez, *Georgia* (B)
Jerry Gray, *Texas* (B)
Tony Thurman, *Boston College* (B)
Rod Brown, *Oklahoma State* (B)
Rick Anderson, *Vanderbilt* (P)

1985 **OFFENSIVE TEAM**
David Williams, *Illinois* (WR)
Willie Smith, *Miami* (TE)
Jim Dombrowski, *Virginia* (T)
Brian Jozwiak, *West Virginia* (T)
Jamie Dukes, *Florida State* (G)
Jeff Zimmerman, *Florida* (G)
Gene Chilton, *Texas* (C)
Chuck Long, *Iowa* (QB)
Bo Jackson, *Auburn* (B)
Lorenzo White, *Michigan State* (B)
Napoleon McCallum, *Navy* (B)
John Lee, *UCLA* (PK)

DEFENSIVE TEAM
Tony Casillas, *Oklahoma* (DL)
Mike Ruth, *Boston College* (DL)
Leslie O'Neal, *Oklahoma State* (DL)
Tim Green, *Syracuse* (DL)
Larry Station, *Iowa* (LB)
Cornelius Bennett, *Alabama* (LB)
Brian Bosworth, *Oklahoma* (LB)
Brad Cochran, *Michigan* (B)
Scott Thomas, *Air Force* (B)
Allan Durden, *Arizona* (B)
David Fulcher, *Arizona State* (B)
Barry Helton, *Colorado* (P)

1986 **OFFENSIVE TEAM**
Chris Carter, *Ohio State* (WR)
Keith Jackson, *Oklahoma* (TE)
John Clay, *Missouri* (T)
Randy Dixon, *Pittsburgh* (T)
Jeff Bregel, *USC* (G)
Jeff Zimmerman, *Florida* (G)
Ben Tamburello, *Auburn* (C)
Vinny Testaverde, *Miami* (QB)
D. J. Dozier, *Penn State* (B)
Brent Fullwood, *Auburn* (B)
Paul Palmer, *Temple* (B)
Jeff Jaeger, *Washington* (PK)

DEFENSIVE TEAM
Jerome Brown, *Miami* (DL)
Tim Johnson, *Penn State* (DL)
Danny Noonan, *Nebraska* (DL)
Reggie Rogers, *Washington* (DL)
Cornelius Bennett, *Alabama* (LB)
Brian Bosworth, *Oklahoma* (LB)
Shane Conlan, *Penn State* (LB)
Thomas Everett, *Baylor* (B)
John Little, *Georgia* (B)
Tim McDonald, *USC* (B)
Garland Rivers, *Michigan* (B)
Bill Smith, *Mississippi* (P)

1987 OFFENSIVE TEAM

Tim Brown, *Notre Dame* (WR)
Keith Jackson, *Oklahoma* (TE)
Dave Cadigan, *USC* (T)
John Elliott, *Michigan* (T)
Mark Hutson, *Oklahoma* (G)
Randall McDaniel, *Arizona State* (G)
Nacho Albergamo, *LSU* (C)
Don McPherson, *Syracuse* (QB)
Gaston Green, *UCLA* (B)
Bobby Humphrey, *Alabama* (B)
Lorenzo White, *Michigan State* (B)
David Treadwell, *Clemson* (PK)

DEFENSIVE TEAM

Chad Hennings, *Air Force* (DL)
Tracy Rocker, *Auburn* (DL)
Daniel Stubbs, *Miami* (DL)
Broderick Thomas, *Nebraska* (DL)
Aundray Bruce, *Auburn* (LB)
Ken Norton Jr., *UCLA* (LB)
Chris Spielman, *Ohio State* (LB)
Bennie Blades, *Miami* (B)
Chuck Cecil, *Arizona* (B)
Deion Sanders, *Florida State* (B)
Jarvis Williams, *Florida* (B)
Tom Tupa, *Ohio State* (P)

1988 OFFENSIVE TEAM

1. Hart Lee Dykes, *Oklahoma State* (WR)
2. Troy Sadowski, *Georgia* (TE)
3. Tony Mandarich, *Michigan State* (T)
4. Pat Tomberlin, *Florida State* (T)
5. Anthony Phillips, *Oklahoma* (G)
6. Mark Stepnoski, *Pittsburgh* (G)
7. John Vitale, *Michigan* (C)
8. Troy Aikman, *UCLA* (QB)
9. Barry Sanders, *Oklahoma State* (RB)
10. Anthony Thompson, *Indiana* (RB)
11. Tim Worley, *Georgia* (RB)
12. Kendall Trainor, *Arkansas* (PK)

DEFENSIVE TEAM

1. Dave Haight, *Iowa* (DL)
2. Bill Hawkins, *Miami* (DL)
3. Mark Messner, *Michigan* (DL)
4. Tracy Rocker, *Auburn* (DL)
5. Mike Stonebreaker, *Notre Dame* (LB)
6. Broderick Thomas, *Nebraska* (LB)
7. Derrick Thomas, *Alabama* (LB)
8. Darryl Henley, *UCLA* (B)
9. Louis Oliver, *Florida* (B)
10. Deion Sanders, *Florida State* (B)
11. Donnell Woolford, *Clemson* (B)
12. Keith English, *Colorado* (P)

1988 OFFENSIVE TEAM

1. 2. 3. 4. 5. 6.

7. 8. 9. 10. 11. 12.

1988 DEFENSIVE TEAM

1. 2. 3. 4. 5. 6. 7. 8. 9. 10. 11. 12.

**After the death of Walter Camp in 1925, Grantland Rice continued selecting Walter Camp All-America teams until 1948. Included above, from 1949 through 1966, are the consensus All-America teams. The Walter Camp Football Foundation resumed the All-America selections in 1967.

WALTER CAMP
PLAYER OF THE YEAR
AWARD WINNERS

1967/1968 O.J. Simpson, *University of Southern California*
1969 Steve Owens, *University of Oklahoma*
1970 Jim Plunkett, *Stanford University*
1971 Pat Sullivan, *Auburn University*
1972 Johnny Rodgers, *University of Nebraska*
1973 John Cappelletti, *Pennsylvania State University*
1974/1975 Archie Griffin, *Ohio State University*
1976 Tony Dorsett, *University of Pittsburgh*
1977 Ken MacAfee, *University of Notre Dame*
1978 Billy Sims, *University of Oklahoma*
1979 Charles White, *University of Southern California*
1980 Hugh Green, *University of Pittsburgh*
1981 Marcus Allen, *University of Southern California*
1982 Herschel Walker, *University of Georgia*
1983 Mike Rozier, *University of Nebraska*
1984 Doug Flutie, *Boston College*
1985 Bo Jackson, *Auburn University*
1986 Vinny Testaverde, *University of Miami*
1987 Tim Brown, *University of Notre Dame*
1988 Barry Sanders, *Oklahoma State University*

1977  1978

1979  1980

1981  1982

1983  1984

1967
1968 1969 1972 1973 1985 1986

1970 1971 1974
1975 1976 1987 1988

WALTER CAMP
COACH OF THE YEAR
AWARD WINNERS

1967 John Pont, *University of Indiana*
1968 Woody Hayes, *Ohio State University*
1969 Glenn (Bo) Schembechler, *University of Michigan*
1970 Robert L. (Bob) Blackman, *Dartmouth College*
1971 Robert S. Devaney, *University of Nebraska*
1972 Joe Paterno, *Pennsylvania State University*
1973 Johnny Majors, *University of Pittsburgh*
1974 Barry Switzer, *University of Oklahoma*
1975 Frank Kush, *Arizona State University*
1976 Frank R. Burns, *Rutgers University*
1977 Lou Holtz, *University of Arkansas*
1978 Warren Powers, *University of Missouri*
1979 John Mackovic, *Wake Forest University*
1980 Vincent J. Dooley, *University of Georgia*
1981 Jackie Sherrill, *University of Pittsburgh*
1982 Jerry Stovall, *Louisiana State University*
1983 Mike White, *University of Illinois*
1984 Joe Morrison, *University of Southern California*
1985 Fisher DeBerry, *U.S. Air Force Academy*
1986 Jimmy Johnson, *University of Miami*
1987 Dick MacPherson, *Syracuse University*
1988 Don Nehlen, *West Virginia University*

1975  1976

1977  1978

1979  1980

1981  1982

1983  1984

1967  1968  1971  1972  1985  1986

1969  1970  1973  1974  1987  1988

WALTER CAMP
MAN OF THE YEAR
AWARD WINNERS

1967 Hamilton Fish, *Harvard University*
1968 Edwin F. "Ted" Blair, *Yale University*
1969 Pete Rozelle, *University of San Francisco*
1970 Harry G. Kipke, *University of Michigan*
1971 Felix A. "Doc" Blanchard, *U.S. Military Academy*
1972 Clinton E. Frank, *Yale University*
1973 Hugh Duffy Daugherty, *Syracuse University, Michigan State University*
1974 Alonzo S. "Jake" Gaither, *Knoxville College, Florida A & M University*
1975 Peter M. Dawkins, *U.S. Military Academy*
1976 Edward W. Krause, *University of Notre Dame*
1977 Fred Dunlap, *Colgate University*
1978 Floyd Little, *Syracuse University*
1979 Jack Kemp, *Occidental College*
1980 Gale Sayers, *University of Kansas*
1981 Otto E. Graham Jr., *Northwestern University*
1982 Merlin Jay Olsen, *Utah State University*
1983 Roger Staubach, *U.S. Naval Academy*
1984 Don Shula, *John Carroll University*
1985 Rocky Bleier, *University of Notre Dame*
1986 Willie D. Davis, *Grambling College*
1987 Levi A. Jackson, *Yale University*
1988 Andy Robustelli, *Arnold College*

1975  1976

1977  1978

1979  1980

1981  1982

1983  1984

1967 1968 1971 1972 1985 1986

1969 1970 1973 1974 1987 1988

WALTER CAMP DISTINGUISHED AMERICAN AWARD WINNERS

1978 James Crowley, *University of Notre Dame*
Donald Miller, *University of Notre Dame*
1979 David A. "Sonny" Werblin, *Rutgers University*
1980 George S. Halas, *University of Illinois*
Alexander M. Haig Jr., *U.S. Military Academy*
1981 Harold "Red" Grange, *University of Illinois*
1982 Edward "Eddie" Robinson, *Grambling State University*
1983 Tom Harmon, *University of Michigan*
1984 Major General William "Bill" Carpenter, *U.S. Military Academy*
1985 Bob Hope
1986 Tom Landry, *University of Texas*
1987 Weeb Ewbank, *Miami University*
1988 Sid Luckman, *Columbia University*
Y. A. Tittle, *Louisiana State University*

1980

1981

1982

1983

1984

1985

1986

1987

1978

1978

1979

1980

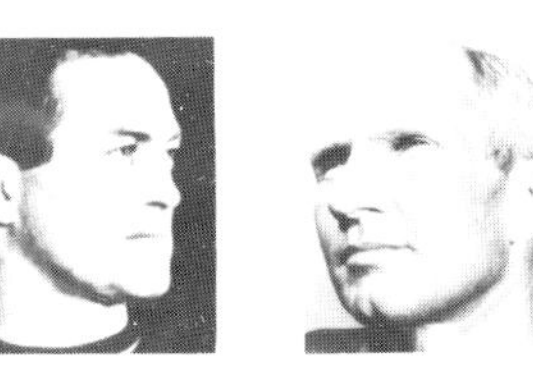
1988 1988

WALTER CAMP ALUMNUS OF THE YEAR AWARD WINNERS

1986 Joe Greene, *North Texas State*
1987 Mike Reid, *Penn State University*
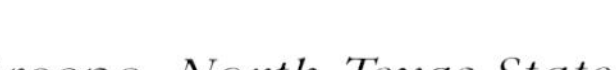
1988 Alan Page, *University of Notre Dame*

1986

1987

1988